Advance Warning

The Rise of Individualism
First Edition

First Edition

Leonard Zagurskie, Jr.

~

Advance Warning, The Rise of Individualism by Leonard Zagurskie, Jr.

Published by Leonard Zagurskie, Jr.

Cover Design by Leonard Zagurskie, Jr.

Editing Assist by Regina Aflleje Zagurskie

First Edition

Printed in the Untied States of America

CONTENTS

Advance Warning – Introduction

This book is an eye-opener which provides insights and a clear understanding of the reality of our society, a commitment to the rights of the individual, our consumer-worker model based economics, its present demise, and a return to the excise tax, tariffs and add the natural resource credit as a viable solution to preserve our way of life, respect individual ownership of capital our individual pursuits of life, liberty and happiness for generations to come.

Western Civilization has not yet economically collapsed, been militarily defeated, or occupied and ruled by a foreign dictator. But Western Civilization is dying. History reports that an economically collapsed people lacking a coherent identity are soon overpowered and dominated. A clear understanding of our past to our present day is critical for our survival as a people and as an individual. We have a genuine Judeo/Christian history that has unsurpassed scientific achievements and advancements. We are the light of the World. If we go down humanity goes down.

In only a short period of time the Federal Congress, President, Federal Agencies and Federal Reserve Board (Feds) will realize that they cannot get the amount of funds, the quantity of money, the magnitude of hard cash that the Feds want, need or require to run their massive federal government from the federal income tax system. Also economic trickery will dwindle, tail off, and diminish to useless nothing, which appearing as nonsense to the American people causes the Feds to lose credibility. There is not enough people working, the wages are decreasing, and more and more folks will be unemployed or working for less money, therefore less and less income tax withholding funds to be paid to the Feds. The day of the mass employer is over, gone, never to return.

If you look back at film footage of the major employers during the 1950's, for example Heinz Ketchup (Pittsburgh, PA) all you see is a multitude of women, wall-to-wall, cooking, processing tomatoes and making ketchup. The same is true for the Detroit auto industry, the motor vehicle assembly plants were massive employers packed full of workers carrying parts from one location to another location, fitting mechanical parts and body parts onto the vehicle's frame as it moves down the assembly line. Check it out, today, in contrast to the 1950's, the motor vehicles, are now, being made without any human being in the vicinity, which is an assembly line production without people. Assembly lines have robotic arms, controlled by computers, which rapidly project out, attach mechanical and vehicle body parts, and simultaneously tightening multiple bolts, with precision that no human being could ever equal. Even the motor vehicle's engine is produced through fully computerized robotic automation, pouring out melting metal, turning, cooling, rotating, processing, then the fully manufactured engine rolls out, through the flapping rubber curtain strips where an inspector can safely view it through a clear plastic glass observation station.

The days of the mass employer are over, gone forever, and correspondingly jobs are on the decrease, and therefore tax revenues are declining, never to return. Hence, the tax revenues from employment income are rapidly decreasing.

Do not think that taxing the "rich" that is the top income producers will counterbalance the tax shortage from the multitudes being out of employment. With the multitudes out of employment there is less purchasing, causing decreasing markets, bringing about less enterprise, then with less enterprise there are less top producers. The enduring top producers will use reserve funds from prosperous times to try to keep an enterprise afloat when the enterprise lacks needed cash flow funds. When these reserve funds are exhausted top producers may get caught short for required loans or tax payments. When expenses rise, sales decrease and cash flow demands are not met, then businesses fail. Without any profit because the unemployed purchase less, the markets dry up, it will not be possible to make loan payments or earn their way out of tax debt. If the top producer would happen to earn more to make loan payments or pay back taxes then more tax debt is owed (increase earnings/increase taxes) going forward in the next taxing period. And, then if the Feds increase the tax rates even more, the increased taxing structure will bring him down, even the most creative, talented hard working enduring top performers will go down under an increasing tax burden during decreasing economic activity.

Eventually the declining tax revenues, resulting from decreased employment income (the source of the Feds tax revenue) will not be enough money for the Feds. Therefore, one would think that the Feds will set up another taxing structure to tax the people to acquire needed federal funding/revenue. In the meantime, no one knows how much economic decline our country will have to undergo until the Feds take action, perhaps before mass chaos, starvation, or that the United States becomes desolate worse than a third world nation. Or if the average folks can survive until the Feds realize that the income tax system is not keeping up (maybe the Feds already knows) and a replacement taxation system is put in place or the Feds expenses are gone, overcome by the events. Undoubtedly, it is clear that the United States is presently headed for a tumultuous major change.

Chapter 1

~

End of an Era
The Consumer Worker Model
The Rise of the Independents

The dominant feature of America of the recent generation, the ending era is that the consumer worker has sustained the economic, social and political structure. The consumer worker model put into practice by Henry Ford is an economic social model that gives workers the power to purchase the products of their own labor. The employer pays the employees enough money to afford to pay the purchase price of products that the Consumer/Workers' labor produces. The idea that the worker could purchase the products of their own labor was novel, never before having taken place in any other past culture, society or government throughout history. The consumer worker model began in the early 1900's in the United States and slightly earlier in Europe, most prominent in Germany. The industrial revolution of the 19th century was revolutionized into the consumer worker model. Out of the 19th century, slavery was abolished and free men were destined to the consumer worker model.

The exploited factory worker became the consumer worker who could now afford all the products produced by consumer workers even a brand new automobile. The fruits of his labor were within his reach. And, in the 1950's and 1960's the consumer worker was afforded or could afford medical and dental care.

To meet the needs and demands of the medical market created to serve the consumer worker and family, the health care industry flourished and responded in growth, expansion and technical advancements and the United States health care system emerged out of our consumer worker model, capital system, entrepreneurship and ingenuity. America's health care system technologically advanced and mass numbers of consumer workers, the people, received the highest quality health care as ever before achieved in any civilization.

The rural farmers became agricultural entrepreneurs unsurpassed in producing crops and livestock with the highest nutritional quality and with the highest yield. To feed the appetite of the consumer workers who could now demand and afford high quality nutritional food gave rise to new industries. These new industries were separate independent enterprises including packaging, distribution, and process improvements. Process improvements like frozen foods are common in today's market. Unfortunately, the dwindling consumer worker model brings about decreases in the buying power and consumer demand, which reduces the market and profits for the American farmers. In addition to the American farmer's decreased market and profit problems, the Feds have added price control and government regulations lowering the price which farmers can sale crops and livestock to the merchants. The Feds' price controls equates to price limitations on the American Farmer. The Feds' price control sets the limit which American farmers can sell crops and livestock products to the merchants on the so called "open market," and presently these price control limits are slashed down below the profit margins of the farmers. Many farmers are surviving by working separate, second jobs, after day-light hours in warehouses or as security guards, and are spending family savings or are borrowing funds just to keep their farms operating, at a loss. Some are managing to keep their farms. Some are losing the family farms. Such price limitations ensure high profits for the merchants, elitists and the self-serving Feds.

6

Also the Feds have slackened the restraints against foreign imported food products allowing the flooding of the market with inferior food products selling below the American market prices. In many states entire areas of farming have been closed down, never to reopen. This is real. The price controls come out of Chicago. Look at the backside of your packaged meats and fish, it may likely read: a product of China, Mexico, and etc. We the American people need the American farmers we must not let this continue. It has to stop.

Here in the United States we have enjoyed living in a self-governing styled democracy, which is a first in the history of mankind. The greatest experiment in government now included a massive labor class that had real influence on the course of events. The American consumer workers by their overwhelming volume of numbers dominated American society, consumer worker buying power then became a source of federal income taxation, a source of financial investing power, which fueled and effected policies and markets, and a modern health care system. America and the consumer worker prospered like no nation ever before.

Americans enjoyed a standard of living never obtained by any other civilization until now. Then, unfortunately, it began to change, over the past thirty years our country experienced three foremost undeniable observable facts:

1.) Technological advancements, engineering, communication, information technology, through computers, robotics and artificial intelligence, an explosion of epic proportion,

2.) Out-sourcing of labor, production and service industry including finance and economics to overseas controlled markets by self-serving business interests, elitists and the Feds,

3.)   Government/political leaders influenced by self-serving political interests lack credibility in the eyes of the American people.

The result now is the dwindling, ever-shrinking, decreasing of the American consumer worker model. The days of the American mass employers are gone. A few "dinosaur" mass employers are left but they are so transformed as to not be viable mass employers. Examples, General Motors and Chrysler are owned by the Feds. The American mass employers are gone: the American consumer worker model is gone.

So we now have a system that is virtually eliminating the consumer worker model. The effects of the demise of the consumer worker model are most evident in the finance, municipality and economic crisis being presently experienced at the time of this writing, by and large now known as the Great Recession. The technological advancements, including computers, robotics and artificial intelligence eliminate the need for mass numbers of employees. Out-sourcing jobs overseas has accelerated the end of the consumer worker model in America. The American consumer worker out of employment, out of money is now out of influence in politics. The previous influence of the consumer worker has been overtaken by elitist influence of self-serving political leaders. What is to come of a system that does not need people (we the people are the consumer workers)?

Without the American consumer worker the system will collapse. The consumer worker is the source of federal income tax, investment capital and health care. The system is imploding, collapsing in on itself. It is like a building imploding by carefully placed dynamite charges by trained demolition experts. The collapse of the system is overdue, it has been delayed by the development of the personal computer revolution of the 1980's, the tech service industry of the 1990's, then the finance service industry of the first decade in 2000, have postponed the economic crash. The present day deferred inflationary Feds' economic policies also can only delay the imploding economy but will not eliminate the impending crash. Of course doing everything now to stop the crash from occurring now is wise, needed and gives us more time. If I can see the system imploding, am I the only one to see this and understand this as a turning point, a major system change, and an end to an era?

If I see and understand the ever-shrinking consumer worker model then there must be others who can see the inevitable collapse. Have the bank bailouts, the Omnibus Act and the Stimulus Act been just for the benefit of the affluent, the elitists, the bankers, the leaders and just these privileged few? Are we on a sinking ship with the captain and crew motoring off with the lifeboats supplies and plunder, abandoning us at sea? Yes, we are looking into the eyes of famine, the collapse of the infrastructure, the loss of many lives and our Country may be lost as well. A remnant always survives. The alternative is the rise of the independents. Those who prepare themselves now will survive. It's not too late. You must prepare now if you are to survive. Also, the time is now to open up real discussions regarding changing the economic system to provide for the American people as well as for preserving the interests of the affluent, elitist and bankers.

Present day economics, simply put is basically through printing more money the Feds resolves debt problems, benefits the affluent, elitists and bankers, which brings about immediate inflation or delayed inflation. Inflation is negative for the people as consumers, consumer workers. A return to the tax system of the American founding fathers, Excise and Tariffs, and a new Natural Resource Credit will restore the American dollar and buying power

9

to the American people and achieve prosperity as made clear and put into plain words in this book.

Rejection of Income Tax
& Property Tax:
A Return to Excise & Tariffs

The fatality of income tax is looming on the near horizon. The elimination of income tax is inevitable and then as a consequence of the elimination of income tax then no more property tax. Income tax and property tax simply no longer work to raise the revenue, necessary for the federal government to repay the national debt. As of the writing of this book, the United States is in debt that is, the national debt is approximately Thirteen (13) Trillion dollars, and of course estimates vary. The United States government owes this debt to China, Japan and the European Union. It is abundantly clear that the Government cannot collect enough income tax from the American citizens to even make the interest payments on the national debt.

The Feds have to borrow even more money or basically print more money (inflation) to make a payment on the national debt. Therefore, the national debt will continue to rise because the principal is not being paid down even if there was not to be any more new spending. And since the federal government appears to be taking on more and more new spending to supposedly make up for short falls and create new jobs the National Debt will continue to rise even more.

It would be expected that the federal government will look to a new source of revenue. Ideas for a national sales tax or a value added tax would be abandoned quickly or simply fail quickly because neither or both of these together will not generate enough money.

The national sales taxes and value added taxes are taxes, which are collected at the purchase of consumer items. Such a national sales taxes and value added taxes are contingent upon individuals earning income to make purchases. Bearing in mind then that income is needed for a national sales tax and/or a value added tax just the same as in the federal income tax. Then such an indirect path to collect tax would clearly generate even less revenue. What then is the federal government to do to raise revenue?

The answer is to return to excise taxes and tariffs. Excise taxes and tariffs were the chief means for raising federal revenue by the founding fathers up until the sixteenth amendment, which was enacted in February 1913. Few people today are familiar with these basic concepts of excise taxes and tariffs.

An "Excise Tax" is a tax on the quantity of goods or services sold. The excise tax is taxed on the quantity or the volume purchased per unit of measure rather than the value of the total sale of the goods or service. For example, 50 cent per gallon of gas. Ten (10) gallons of gas, then five (5) dollars excise tax. The real revenue generator for the federal government will be generated through tariffs.

A "Tariff" tax is a government tax on imports or exports. Tariffs also level the playing field for our homeland's industry.

When the federal government extracts tariffs from the foreign importers then that cost is added to the cost of the sale price. When the cost of foreign imports goes up it becomes profitable for America to produce the products here in America. Also specifically enacting a tariff tax on China, Japan and the European Union proportionately to the debt owed to these countries by the Feds will act as an offset to the Feds' debt. An offset can be calculated to make a matching offset payment on these countries respective debts. And the excise tax is collected before the foreign products are unloaded, uncrated onto our docks. Then the risk of selling these products in America for profit falls on the importer. Instead of inflation on the American people the tariff tax shifts the burden on foreigners importing goods or services.

Income Tax Expansion
Into The Consumer Worker
Model
& Protecting Old Money

Do not be deceived or mistaken. The United States is at a crossroads with one path leading the people off a cliff. It is written, "How my people suffer from lack of knowledge." You need to know about the consumer worker model and the income tax creation and expansion: The crossroads we are facing is either to continue to empower the people to make individual choices, to achieve, to discover one's own destiny or to give that power to government to act as the caregiver, regulator and custodian of our rights to pursue life, liberty and happiness from cradle to grave. And, for many the result will be an early grave: A grave due to death by famine.

On September 17, 1787, the Constitution of the United States of America, was enacted, our country started out as our promoter and protector of the individual and there was no federal income tax. The first one hundred twenty-six (126) years of this Country followed the original intent of the Constitution, that being no income tax. The source of funds for the federal government was "Excise" and "Tariff" taxes.

Then after the Industrial Revolution occurred roughly between 1760 and 1830, and after the Civil War occurred from 1861to 1865 the federal income tax was first started in 1913. The 16th amendment did not become constitutional law until February 1913 allowing income to be taxed.

This first income tax was directed only at the highest income producers the top two "2" percent in 1916. Not the most wealthiest, but the highest income producers were targeted: A very important distinction. The highest two 2 percent income producers were individuals earning over $1,000,000 and they were taxed at seventy-seven percent (77.0%), in 1918. High-income producers would be eliminated from accumulating wealth. Hence they could not compete with those who had already acquired their wealth. Those who had already acquired their wealth, those with massive wealth, not only mega money, but also had vast holdings of land, and the control of the means of production, buildings, timber, commercial and industrial markets, communications, railroads all acquired during the Industrial Revolution and the Civil War pay no income tax. It is referred to as "Old Money."

Old Money does not pay income tax on their accumulated money/wealth. Taxing interest earned on principal is minimal and does not affect Old Money. Old Money has been protected ever since. Income tax rates continued to rise and enlarged the range of income producers to include middle-income producers. Review the charts provided by the IRS in the later in this book or online at the IRS website. The wealthy whom already had accumulated extensive wealth were protected from the competition of any new high-income producers because the new high-income producers had their profit taken from them as income tax. Old Money, who were the wealthiest (accumulated before income taxation) were guaranteed to stay the wealthiest because taxing income guaranteed Old Money's place on top of our society because our society is primarily a capitalistic economic society and Old Money had the capital (the money the wealth).

Then after the development of the Consumer Worker Model the Federal Income Tax expanded to include taxing the income of the average worker. Mandatory Federal Tax withholding was established in 1943, and sustained thereafter. Now the workers were having their income taxed and that tax was being extracted from the people at the moment it was earned. Old Money's wealth was protected against taxation, remember its not income. In 1945 the top tax rate for those making over $200,000 was 94.0%. Now that is wealth protection from any new high-income producer ever taking the social place of Old Money. Never in the history of the world has a government taxed its own people as in America today.

From Division of Labor
To Loss of Economic Power

First we need to recognize that United States is a unique experiment in the empowerment of the individual. The history of world civilizations is a history of Kings, Dictators and Tyrants with absolute power over the people. The division of labor made civilization possible, powered by slave labor and serf labor. Henry Ford's consumer worker produced our present day economic structure where the consumer workers can consume the products of their work. The economic power to purchase consumer goods is the basis, the foundation and the underpinning of empowerment of the individual workers, the people now, today. Therefore, if the people lose the basis of their economic power the people lose their political power. Allowing the present policies, which allows the elimination of consumer workers with high technology production, eliminates the economic power, the political power and the need for us people in this society. Without being needed, without economic power and without political power we may have to resort to begging the government not to abandon us in the day of famine in a collapsed economic and social system and we will abandon any thoughts of our rights to pursue life, liberty and happiness.

High Tech Production
Return to Excise Taxes & Tariffs
&
Introduction of the Natural Resource Credit

Today there are few new jobs and fewer old jobs. The day of the mass employer is past history. Technology, which is highly advanced, now does the work. The government spending money to make jobs cannot be successful. The Government takes then the Government gives. The Government spending money to make jobs is equivalent to taxing the people so the Government has money to pay "someone" to pay the people to work. Government spending money to make jobs ends up being a bailout of the banks in any economic crisis. What will happen to the people?

It is here today. Technology, highly advanced with computers, robotics, artificial intelligence, and fully automated assembly lines, that is "high technology production" or "high tech" (for short) we have developed a society that does not need people. We are these people. Our society resulted from the rise of the consumer worker out of the industrial revolution. And, our present day economics is based on the consumer worker model, initiated by Henry Ford at the beginning of the last century. Then back in the 1950's and 1960's production was labor intensive. For example, several workers carried a car door to the frame of the car and held it up to the frame while another worker wrenched bolts by hand attaching the door to the frame. In factories multitudes of workers through out the United States were needed for massive labor intensive assembly type work. Today there are no such workers, in their place are automated assembly lines, robotic arms, programmed by computers, which do all the work. Car production as well as production of all other consumer products is high technology production. Therefore, this high technology production eliminates the consumer worker.

Eliminating the consumer workers also eliminates our present day economics because our economy is dependent upon the consumer workers purchasing power, i.e., the consumer worker consuming, borrowing, and spending money and the income tax funds collected from the consumer worker. If our society becomes a society that does not need consumer workers, it will also be a society that does not need the people, because high tech does the work instead of the people, then the present economics cannot provide for the people because of a lack of consumer workers' purchasing power and a lack of income tax funds collected from the consumer worker. Such a society and economy then that does not need or provide for its people will collapse. What will replace such a society is at the crossroads in front of us today.

I advocate continuing to empower the people as individuals to the right to pursue life, liberty and happiness and to increase the spiritual, political, social and economic strength of individuals and communities by the following:

1.) Immediately cease all income taxes and real property taxes on American citizens. Return to Excise and Tariff taxes.

2.) Develop and institute the Natural Resource Credit.

3.) Providing electricity to all American citizens no payment required.

4.) American Consumer Workers immediately commence rebuilding the electrical grids, placing all distribution cables underground. Underground cables are safer, protected from the elements and eliminates the blot on the landscape of telephone poles and wires from the view of our beautiful country. Configuring mini-grids to distribute electricity to self-sufficient local communities, avoiding the inefficient mega grids.

Such actions will immediately cause a shock wave of prosperity in United States and can be accomplished with respecting the ownership of capital and wealth of private individuals in United States by return to Excise Tax (tax on volume of goods sold, similar to sales tax, but less) and Tariff taxes (tariff is a tax on imports, tariff/tax on foreign imports which will offset, that is, corresponds to the Feds' foreign debt payments), and amending the currency and monetary statutes to provide for full payment on demand or credit to the owners of natural resource leases and franchise through a natural resource credit to restore value to the American dollar.

The following is the basics of the natural resource credit. The natural resource credit computes the value of the resources as it is extracted from the land and then subtracts or expends credits at the point of usage as kilowatts of electricity passing through the consumers' meter. The idea is the simple balance sheet. Credits counted and recorded as extracted from the land are then subtracted or expended when spent by consumers. Although the consumer would pay absolutely zero to the electric company, the natural resource credits would be recorded as spent at usage meters to provide for an accurate distribution of the natural resource credits to the owners of leases and franchises and the balance as amounts for tax to the federal government. Credits coming into the Fed general funds would compensate for the Feds' overprinting the money, restore the value of the dollar and offset inflation. The Feds would be responsible for overseeing the economics, security and maintenance of the grids. The natural resource credits would be exchangeable, payable and backed in full force and charge by the American dollar.

American Owned
Natural Resources

The funds from revenues, profits and taxes from the sale of American owned natural resources should be used towards funding our federal taxes after first paid to us the American people in the form of "Free Electricity." This free electricity would not require any payment by consumers. However, the owners of the leases and franchises to natural resources would be fully compensated through the natural resource credit. This free electricity to American people is essential to our society after the end of the consumer worker model. After the end of the consumer worker model there will be minimal to zero employment. Therefore, consumers will have little money to pay for electricity, needed for heat, basic subsistence and enterprising undertakings. With these changes the American people will have a chance to come back, small businesses, self-employment, independence and with ingenuity return as a foremost society and preserve our heritage, our way of life, respecting individual ownership of capital our individual pursuits of life liberty and happiness for generations to come, and the Feds will get their funds.

I am advocating that the American natural resources should be the property of the American people not the bureaucrats, wealthy landowners and oil companies. If you own your home you can check your deed and your state law then you will probably find out that you do not own the mineral, gas or oil rights underneath your property. I am not alone in advocating natural resources should be the property of the people. The State of Alaska Permanent Fund Dividend, Alaska state law, distributes to the people of Alaska state refunds paid from the sale, profits and taxes of the State's oil.

State Property Laws and deed reservations have created big winners and big losers in the profits from American natural resources. The big winners are the elitists. The big losers are the American people. The American natural resources are owned by State Commissions/State Land Divisions or mammoth landowners. Long-standing state laws, many from the 1970's, have split mineral/gas rights from the surface of real estate to the ownership of the state. Mineral/gas rights are rights to the subsurface mineral/gas located under a piece of real property. These mineral/gas rights by state statutes were either conveyed to State Commissions/State Land Divisions or reserved in deeds by earlier landowners (split out and kept by the earlier landowners) on public record. State laws vary. You can get state property law specifics by consultation with an attorney licensed in your state. A proper title exam will reveal whether these rights exist and how they will affect the current or future ownership on a particular piece of property. The State Land Commissions or Land Divisions are responsible for managing State-owned mineral and gas rights and administering the program for leasing rights for oil and gas exploration, production and profit. Result, a few get the mammoth share of the monetary benefits of the American natural resources and the American people are mailed the utility bill.

Mega Power Plants
& Local Community Plants

Have you ever have had the opportunity to see first hand the tall high-tension lattice structured high-voltage electric power transmission towers with the long spans of electric cable wire traveling a vast distance from tower to tower. This is typically referred to as electricity distribution. Electricity distribution is bulk transfer of electrical energy, from nuclear and/or coal fired generating plants far away, often to out of state population centers, where transformers reduce the high voltage transmission strength electricity down to a power level for usage in the consumer household. These high voltage transmission lines, run like the spokes out of the hub of a wheel and are called the high voltage transmission networks, and typically are referred to as "power grids" or sometimes simply as "the grid".

North America has three major grids: The Western Grid; The Eastern Grid and the Texas grid. Historically, the same company owned the transmission and distribution lines, but over the last decade "reforms" have divided up the pie, the business into more service providers. Therefore more that just a few fat cats (elitists) get all the proceeds from the customer electricity bills.

If you have not personally viewed these tall electric towers with vast spans of wire that travel very long distances (typically greater than 400 miles) you need to look personally down the tall tower to tall tower lines for as far as the eye can see to the horizon and then you need to wonder just how much electricity is being lost in pushing this high voltage power through this grid to its far away destinations. If for example a car battery was hooked up with a cable running back and forth just between the distance of two towers all the battery power would be lost in the resistance of the

Advance Warning, The Rise of Individualism

electric wire. Resistance is simply a physical characteristic of wire that decreases the energy of the electricity. The more wire the more loss of electric energy. Extensive lengths of wire cause extensive amounts of lost electric energy. The power companies respond that electricity is transmitted at high voltages and low amperage to minimize the energy lost in the long distance transmission. However enormous amounts of energy are clearly being lost in the hundreds of miles of high-tension electric wire grid and there is no feasible way to reduce the resistance. For example silver is a better conductor of electricity than copper. But the price of silver prohibits its use. The clear way to reduce all the loss of energy from hundreds of miles of cable is simply not to have hundreds of miles of cable at all, instead have all the power produced locally thus avoiding all the loss of electrical energy caused by hundreds of miles of cable. Shifting to locally produced electricity would immediately save energy, create new jobs and also eliminate the looming catastrophe of the electric grid failure.

   The grid was built back in the 1950's and 1960's. It is vulnerable to failure due to a high consumer demand for air condition in a heat wave or possible electric heat demands in an extremely cold prolonged weather, or destruction by high winds or by terrorist attack. Individual communities could have mini-nuclear power plants, which once built and fueled could provide safe energy to the local community and no one would pay an electric bill. Again any owners of leases or natural resource capital would be compensated with natural resource credits. These individual community power plants should be built immediately while the old grid is still functional. The community power plants should utilize a new electrical grid distribution with all distribution cables underground. Underground cables are safer. Underground distribution cables are protected from the weather elements therefore no down wires due to wind, snow/ice or mud slides. Employed consumer workers building new community plants and

28

electrical grids, receiving compensation, therefore, will increase purchasing, boosting overall economic activity and increase tax revenues for the Feds. The natural beauty of American landscapes is superior without unsightly telephone poles and wires. The enhanced aesthetic value of American landscapes is a priceless benefit to all.

Chapter 2

~

How to Understand our Society Maturing of Capitalism The Logical Process

Essential to understanding any subject matter begins with knowledge of its past, its history in order to understand the subject matter in its totality as a whole then distinguishing and identifying the components that make up the entirety. A clear understanding of our society then starts then with its history then examining the components that combine to make up the whole. The behavior of the whole system cannot be determined by the behavior of its separate parts. Graphing out the trends of the whole system exposes the fate of the individual components.

Capitalism High Ideals

The maturing of capitalism allows capitalism to achieve its most renowned ideals, such as individualism, freedom, virtue and representative government recognized in the founding of our country. These high ideals in the forming of our government include that individuals should be free to pursue Judeo/Christian beliefs and their own enterprises, and that, in a republican form of government, individuals pursuing their Judeo/Christian beliefs and individual specialty of work will guarantee the interests of the society as a whole.

   In the first civilizations such as Ancient Israel, Phoenicia and the Nile Delta, in particular ancient Egypt, leading up to the days of Moses the civilizations were able to develop a division of labor, for example the benefit of the seasonal overflow of the Nile River which fertilized the farming lands. These highly fertilized farm lands allowed farming which produced an abundance of food, a food source plenty for all to benefit from, thus freeing up the manpower to allow others to specialize into tradesmen, craftsman, military warriors, scribes and learned occupations involving high standards of intellectual knowledge after education and training. Today we have so much more, we have the technological factors, computers, robotics, and fully automated assembly lines, artificial intelligence, information technologies, communications and our countries vast natural resources are a source for further freeing up manpower and allowing further specialization, social advancement, intellectual knowledge and scientific achievement. The prosperity of the American people would not only surpass the golden age of King Solomon's Israel but also surpass the golden age of the consumer worker by reining in a new era that elevates and empowers the individual, while respecting the capital wealth already acquired and resolving the deficiencies of the Fed's economics.

The Development of the Consumer Worker Production of Goods Economics

Economics, the study of the production/distribution of goods and the management of wealth, by a country, household, or business enterprise has to be derived out of other areas of knowledge. In other words, economics is a viewpoint that separates the production/distribution of goods and management of wealth from other concerns, such as politics, sociology, religion, ethics, and etc. In the capital system value is fair market value. Fair market value is what an able, capable buyer will pay for something in the market place. In Marxism, value is how much work, that is, how much human effort was expended in the production of an item. The capitalist definition of value is visibly more superior to Marxism in light of high technology. For example, an item in the market place with substantial importance to consumers when produced entirely from a computerized machine would have zero value under Marxism.

The fundamental unit of meaning in capitalist and economics is the item, that is, consumer worker capitalism relies on the creation of a consumer culture, a large segment of the population that is not producing most of what it is consuming. Since capitalism, like mercantilism, is fundamentally based on distributing goods— moving goods from one place to another—consumers have no social relation to the people who produce the goods they consume. In earlier non-capitalist societies, such as clans, tribal or extended family societies, people had real social relations to the producers of the goods they consumed, such as tent makers, carpenters, potters, and farmers. But when people do not have social relations with those who make the items they consume, then that means the only relation they have is with the item itself. So part of capitalism as a way of culture is that people become "consumers," that is, they define themselves more by the objects they purchase (consume) rather than the objects they produce.

For the capitalist economic growth is to steadily become wealthier. The accumulation of the means of production (the instrumentality, materials, land, tools) as property is called capital and the property-owners of these means of production are the capitalists. Productive labor falls under the control of the capitalist. The means of production and labor is influenced, managed, used, or controlled by the capitalist using rational calculations in order to realize increasing profits. In America the consumer worker model has enabled the capitalist to accumulate vast capital and acquire extensive financial strength to generate future profits with exponential growth returns. Capitalism has exhausted the consumer worker model in America and has moved its economic activity abroad for increasing profits. In order to restore the consumer worker model, and return the capitalists to realize profit in America, America needs to add the natural resource credit to the consumer worker model and return to excise taxes and tariffs and end employment income tax. Capitalism, then as a revitalized ongoing economic activity with increased economic growth and increased profit will not only benefit the consumer worker and the capitalist but also the Feds will benefit as well with increased tax revenue. The capitalist and the consumer workers implementing the natural resource credit are providing for a new economic revival and growth in America.

The Feudal System
The Capital System
The Consumer Worker Model
& The Rise of the Independents

The period of the consumer worker followed two major events in the history of the capital system and a third major event is unfolding in front of our eyes. You are in the middle of economic and political struggles and warfare. The basic structure is a capitalist system, a democratic government under the rule of law. The politicians follow the dollar and strive to rule. The capitalists strive to merchandize, and obtain and control more capital.

The capitalist system started out in the feudal system, Lords, Vassals and Serfs. The first major event that occurred was that the Civil War ended slavery. The second major event that occurred was that Henry Ford, founder of Ford Motors put into practice the consumer worker economy.

The Consumer Worker Model simply put is where the workers are paid enough to afford to purchase consumer products that their labor or the labor of other workers were capable of producing. Henry Ford paid workers enough compensation to afford motor vehicles and other consumer products that their families needed. The consumer worker economy replaced the earlier agrarian society, short-lived industrial tycoon system and earlier episodes of the feudal system. Ending the former cold reality of the old saying that "the cobbler's (shoe maker's) children have no shoes" – previously the cobblers could not afford shoes for their children! Thus, enters the consumer worker model. Other capitalists of the Henry Ford era vehemently opposed Henry Ford for expanding the franchise to purchase such items as otherwise available only to the affluent, wealthy, elitist capitalist to the availability of the multitudes of consumer workers. Nonetheless expanding the consumer market to the reach of the workers tremendously benefited the elitist capitalists because an expanded market meant increased profits. These consumer items previously only available to the privileged few were now generally available for the enjoyment by the workers who produced the items. The purchasing power of the privileged few was now available to the millions of consumers in the working class, thus the market for the capitalist was likewise expanded to the millions of consumer workers. The consumer market territory expanded after World War Two from America and Europe throughout South America, Asia and Australia placing unprecedented wealth, capital, power and control into the hands of the elitist capitalist. And if that was not enough, additionally this expanded consumer market exploded into a global financial market adding correspondingly unprecedented wealth capital, power and control into the hands of the elitist capitalist.

Why do we feel ripped-off? We are capitalist subjects and American citizens. A capitalist is one who owns "Capital", controls the raw resources, the means and instrumentation of production, the buildings, the property and the merchandising of the finished products. We live and work in a capitalist society. However, the majority of Americans do not have Capital. We support and participate in the capitalist system. But we are not entitled to rights, privileges or protections under the capitalist system. We are capitalist subjects. We subject ourselves to the employment authority and control for the employment opportunities, compensation and benefits provided. As American citizens we are entitled to rights, privileges and/or protections under our democratic government. After the first great depression the consumer worker class was provided with protections under the "New Deal" legislation. We basically have the New Deal legislation rights, privileges and protections enacted into laws, basically, Social Security Retirement, Labor Laws and Banking Securities laws. Also as American citizens we have employment and unemployment law protections and workers compensation benefits, which are dwindling away.

Two Extraordinary Events
Last Century America

The two most important events which have occurred in the last hundred years in America is the consumer/worker concept put into practice by Henry Ford and the avoidance of an all out military conflict with the former Soviet Union. One created a class of consumer/workers, of which such consumer/workers could afford and acquire the types of products that their productive efforts produce. Such a consumer/worker class had never existed before. Not in Western Society, King David/King Solomon, Phoenicia, Ancient Egypt, Greece, Rome, the British Empire, and also including up through the industrial revolution in America. All these former societies developed a large class of individuals, which enjoyed the benefits of the labor and the increased technology of the times.

Advance Banking 101 Western Civilization & The Natural Resource Credit

The consumer worker model needed a new banking system. The banking system based on the gold standard functioned effectively for the kings and the vassals of the feudal system. But was insufficient for the consumer worker models because an individual bank would fail, collapse moreover shut down when there was a "run on the bank." The Federal Reserve Banking system promised answers, progressed from a gold standard, silver certificates, bank bailouts to the now economics called "velocity of money". I advocate the natural resource credit system.

Almost all banks up through the 1880's were national banks, chartered by the federal government and were allowed by law to issue their own currency in the form of bank notes. Bank notes were limited, determined by the supply of gold, which was on deposit held in that individual bank. Additionally the banks received deposits from the people in the consumer checking and savings accounts. The consumer worker model brought into existence mass numbers of consumers making mass numbers of deposits into the banks, which far surpassed the banks' deposits on hold of gold, which determined, limited the amount of currency the bank could issue. The money from the checking and savings accounts would then be the source of money to make loans to the consumers at large, for example, mortgages, only a small amount of cash then was kept on-hand in the bank vaults.

A run on the bank would occur when the people, the consumer workers, the depositors in mass numbers would line up at the bank to request withdraws from their accounts. At a certain point, the bank would not have the money to hand to the consumer standing in the line at the counter who was requesting a withdraw. Not being able to make payment on demand is the straightforward definition of bank failure.

The answer was The Federal Reserve Act, passed in 1913. The Federal Reserve Act was a bankers' utopia because the consequence of a bank failure was passed onto the American taxpayer. Today, the euphemism is, that is, the harsh, blunt term, which calls it as it really is, is Bank Bailouts. A bank run, a mass multitudes of consumer withdraw requests of money, which would surpass the amount of money actually in the vault and exceeding the amount the bank could issue though gold reserves, would then be absorbed by the United States taxpayers.

Times were very good for many Americans up through the1920s. Millions of consumer workers began to purchase stock through the stock market, however the consumer workers paid more for the stock than the stock was worth. Consumer workers continued to invest money in the stocks as the prices continued to inflate. The consumer workers believed that their stocks were dramatically increasing in value. But unfortunately for the economy, and so many consumer workers the stock market sold stocks dramatically inflated in price. In essence, stocks were selling for more money than they were worth. The stock market grew exponentially then in 1929 the skyrocketed stock market rapidly deflated in value as investors and everyone realized that the stocks were inflated in price. In 1929, the frenzy stopped. Black Tuesday set off the stock market crash, which led to the Great Depression of the 1930's.

The gold standard had to be eliminated, extinguished, and thoroughly wiped out in order for President Roosevelt and Congress to re-inflate the U.S. economy during the middle to late 1930s. By Executive Order 6102, signed on April 5, 1933, by President Franklin D. Roosevelt, the President took the nation off the gold standard, requiring all gold owned by the consumer workers to be delivered to the government under penalty of large fines and/or jail sentences. The government melted the majority of the gold, which raised gold's value by nearly seventy-five percent (75%). To maintain an appearance of credibility in the Federal Reserve Note, the United States money, silver became the replacement standard. Starting in 1933 there was rapid proliferation of over issuances of Silver certificates. Silver certificates continued to be over issued through March 1964, which was halted by the Secretary of the Treasury, C. Douglas Dillon under John F Kennedy.

The present economic concept, velocity of money coupled with the quantum theory of money is to provide the money as needed in the national economy. Money is a unit of measure and as more consumer workers labor earning money, depositing money, exchanging the money for consumables, as well as banks loaning money to consumer workers to finance purchases, so goes the velocity of money. The velocity of money (also known as the velocity of circulation) is the average frequency with which a unit of money is spent in a specific period of time. The quantum (quantity/ amount) theory (supply and demand) of money relates changes in price to changes in the quantity of money. Therefore the Federal Reserve Board theoretically controlling the printing of money controls inflation and deflation.

In 2009 and 2010 the Federal Reserve Board exercised Quantitative easing (QE) a monetary policy to stimulate the economy. The money is "digitized" not printed. The central bank issues (creates) money, transfers it as bonds to the banks, then electronically buys back its own government bonds at a discount resulting in a yield (additional money) left behind at the bank as profit for the bank or electronically purchases at a discount other financial assets, in order to increase the money supply and the money reserves of the banks, which also raises the value of the purchased financial assets.

This is all well and good for the Bankers. But again, as in the fall of 2009 the bankers, and Wall Street received bailouts while the consumer workers' 401K retirement account and pension funds tanked out and the consumer worker received zero.

The economic system is working for the elitists but it is not working for the consumer worker. The Feds use a misleading analogy of "injecting" money into the economy. The Feds supposedly "inject" money into a slow national economy to speed it up. The theory is that money is printed and "injected" into the national economy for an increase in the velocity of the national economy. The misleading analogy implies as a needle injects into an arm that printed money is injected into the economy. However, money not owned by any particular person or entity has no power. If for example one million dollars is put into any bank vault then who would be authorized to spend it? Money must be owned to have any spending power. Moving past the basics, past the theoretical, the answer is that money is injected, that is, newly printed money is put into the hands of elitist banker executives, by means of zero present interest or low interest rate loans or bonds from the Federal Reserve Board. Then the Feds buys back the loans at a slightly higher rate, leaving the difference behind as profit for the Elitist banker. At times these "loans" are done instantly by electronic deposits and returns, that is called digitizing money. A one percent increase in the buy back of federal loans results in a fortune when it is one percent of an enormous amount of funds. The power of money is in authorizing the spending of the money and such power of the money is in the hands of the elitist banker executives. In 2009 approximately 2 Trillion Dollars was transferred by means of zero percent interest discount rate loans to elitist banker executives.

The system is effective for the elitists but it is failing for the consumer worker. The technological factors, the computers, robotics, artificial intelligence and a political policy to outsource American jobs, along with an economic system that takes care of only the most well to do of our society, the elitist banker executives is a societal system that will come crashing down as it has in the past unless it is changed now. The industrial revolution was transformed, changed from the blighted factories, destitute workers, suffering sweatshops, men, women and children laboring endless hours without human dignity, to the consumer worker model where the multitudes, the masses where able to purchase consumer goods as of the same kind they labored to produce, resulting in a framework for self-development, self-worth, self-fulfillment and dignity. If the industrial revolution could transform and become the consumer worker model then of course the economics can transform respecting the ownership of capital and wealth of private individuals in United States providing full credit to the owners of such capital through a natural resource credit.

The natural resource credit would bring about extensive prosperity in United States providing electricity to consumers, paying credits to the owners of these assets based on the volume of consumer usage and supplying financial funding into the Fed general tax funds, off-setting inflation and increasing the velocity of money.

1.) Presently when one makes a deposit into the bank, that deposit is credited as a liability because the bank owes the money to the holder of the account. When the money is loaned out as for a mortgage it is credited as an asset because it is owed to the bank.

2.) When the Federal Reserve Bank "injects" or loans money at a zero percent interest, the banker receiving the money, credits it as a liability because the money is owed to the Federal Reserve Bank.

3.) When the Bank loans out this money obtained from the Federal Reserve Bank to the American people, the bank gets interest.

4.) Then when the bank pays the money back to the Fed at a discount rate the bank gains the profit of the discount, and that discount, the cost of this federal debt, is passed on as inflation to the American people, consumer workers.

5.) The extraction of the natural resources, raw materials, which occur naturally within the American environment, the minerals, gas, oil, energy, land, timber, water, would be credited as an asset to the American people as they are extracted, because the natural resources are owned by the American people, consumer workers.

6.) The natural resource credit would first pay the electricity bill of the American consumers, next the credits would pay the capital owners of the leases/franchises of natural resources, then the remainder of credits would be paid as funds for federal tax revenues, the effect being the opposite of inflation (deflation), would restore the value of the dollar.

7.) Crediting the usage of natural resources as a liability would result in a better reflection of value and serve as an additional guard against inflation.

8.) The natural resource credit simply provides for accounting that takes the consumer workers' interests into consideration, allowing for "free electricity" as crediting for the natural resources as assets owned by the American people, as well as compensation for labor expended in extracting, processing and distribution of the products of our natural resources, not just the interests of the elitist banker executives, and which, also respects the ownership of capital and wealth of private individuals in United States.

The natural resource credit provides for a society that requires people, and it is possible in our era of computers, technology, robotics, artificial intelligence, and fully automated assembly lines. If we fail to address this issue as a nation, our society will collapse and we submit our general welfare and destiny to those who will govern us.

Americans Have
Not Always Paid Income Taxes

The Feds can survive without our income tax dollars. The federal income tax has not always been a part of the American taxation system. The Constitution prohibited income tax because it was a direct tax. It was not envisioned by the founding fathers. Under the Constitution of the United States it was clear that income tax was unconstitutional. If high-income producers were taxed on their income then those who already had wealth would be protected from any new competition. The founding fathers did not want America to produce an Aristocracy that is a rich ruling class. Protecting those who already had wealth and capital from those who were working to earn income was clearly not an objective of the Constitution. Rather the goal was for leaders to spring up from the people.

So then, except for an attempt by President Lincoln to raise money during the Civil War the source of funds for the federal government was "Excise" and "Tariff" taxes. A "Excise Tax" is a tax on a specific good or service, regularly imposed on the quantity purchased rather than the value. Examples are gasoline taxes, cigarette taxes, and telecommunications taxes. Tax per gallon, tax per package, etc. A "Tariff" tax is a government tax on imports or exports. Tariffs raise the prices of imported goods, thus leveling the playing field with American produced products, which are subject to massive federal, state and local regulations whereas such regulations are minimal or non-existent in the market of the importing foreign country.

Income tax started in 1894 when it was buried in the fine print of the repetitive annual tax language of the Wilson-Gorman Tariff Act of 1894. Slipped into the Wilson-Gorman Tariff Act of 1894 was inserted brief language to tax "on income" and the rates. The new income tax was directed at the Americans earning the most income. The income tax was collected by the newly formed Internal Revenue Service. Charles Pollock a Massachusetts citizen was taxed and he challenged the tax. Then in 1895 the Supreme Court of the United States ruled in his favor in "<u>Pollock v. Farmers' Loan & Trust Company</u>" that income taxes levied by the Wilson-Gorman Tariff Act were direct taxes therefore <u>unconstitutional</u>. Next to over rule the Supreme Court and allow the income tax the Sixteenth Amendment was ratified in 1913. There is strong historical evidence that the 16th amendment was not legally ratified. This extensive evidence of fraud is available for viewing on the Internet. Through fraud on the states with various documents which circulated with varying tax language including documents, which, fully omitted the term "on income", the Amendment "passed".

If United States has operated under funding through excise and tariffs, then why the push to tax the income of the most productive members of our society? Those pushing the income tax were known as "Progressives." President Woodrow Wilson was the most prominent progressive. As a professor, then as president at Princeton he is recognized today as one of the founders of the discipline of political science. The Progressive Era was also a period marked by the growth of racism, eugenics, and white supremacist policies. President Wilson introduced segregation of employees into the federal government.

Clearly taxing income stops individuals from earning wealth and protects those who already have wealth and capital. Taxing the rich means taxing only those working to acquire income. Those who already have the wealth and capital get to keep all their wealth and capital unless their capital produces income, then the income is taxed. Clearly the idea in 1894 was to keep the wealthiest at the time the wealthiest families from there on out by preventing any one else from obtaining enough of wealth to be an elitist capitalist who could control the raw resources, the means and instrumentation of production, the buildings, the property and the merchandising of the finished products.

This protectionism of wealth from 1894 families is evidenced in the federal income tax rates history. Since the income tax has been constitutionalized the number of years that the top tax rate has equaled or exceeded **fifty percent** of individual top end income is **fifty-six (56) years.** The following is extracted from the federal income tax rates history, it provides the history of the top rate changes by the years:

Year/Years	Top Rate	Year/Years	Top Rate
1913	6%	1946	91 %
1916	15%	1944	94 %
1918	77%	1964	77%
1919	73%	1965	70%
1921	58%	1982	50%
1925	25%	1987	38.5%
1932	63%	1988	28 %
1936	79%	1991	31%
1941	81%	1993	39.6%
1942	88%	2002	38.6%
1944	94 %	2003	35%

Chapter 3

~

Can't you see what is happening to the American People?

Can't you see what is happening to the American people? You know whom I am talking about. Folks, who work or want to work for a living, buy cars, get married, raise children, pay bills and maybe buy a house.

Not enough time, not enough money & feeling bamboozled and ripped off.

When one hears the news of the actions of our elected representatives and Wall Street one cannot help but to wonder if one is fairly and adequately being represented. The needs and concerns of the American people seem to simply being given lip service then ignored. The Feds have literally gone through over $17 Trillion Dollars and we have nothing to show for it. No new hospitals, no new electrical power plants and no more or new military assets, such as aircraft carriers, new weapons or defensive military systems. The Chinese do! The new J-20 jet stealth fighter, which is larger than the U.S. stealth planes, allowing more room to carry more and yet it can fly longer than the U.S. stealth planes. Excuse me. But just where did all this $17 Trillion Dollars go! Whereas the needs and concerns of Wall Street are given first priority including massive $700 billion and $800 billion cash infusions. What about retirees, pensioners, 401K Plans and the

American family providers? What about the American workers and homeowners what is going to happen to us? You need to understand where you fit in and what is going on so you can take better care of yourself and your family. Perhaps help others. But even if you can do nothing, at least you will know what is going on and what will happen to you. You can tell others about excise tax, tariffs and the natural resource credit and maybe enough of people can persuade the Feds to listen to us. And, we can help the Fed get the money they need.

You Only Hear
What They Want You to Hear

An estimated 14 million people died of starvation, mostly in the Ukraine but also in the North Caucasus, Kazakhstan and Russia in the early 1930's and this is not taught in the schools or the universities until maybe if just recently. But this fact is easily verified on the Internet.

The war in Iraq ended on January 1, 2009, which is referred to in Iraq as Sovereignty Day, now a national holiday in Iraq. In Iraq there was a national commemoration observance of the End of the Iraq War. On January 1, 2009, Iraq took formal control of the Green Zone, the fortified enclave that once served as the headquarters of the Coalition Provisional Authority. The walls of the majestic Republican Palace in Baghdad's Green Zone were stripped bare. The vaults that secured American cash and classified documents are gone, and the cement blast walls that protected the front entrance were taken down. The U.S. military dining facility inside which was once the American Embassy served its last meal New Year's Eve. The airspace formally was transferred from American to Iraqi control. The new security framework also gave the Iraqi government primary jurisdiction over the contractors. There was no broadcast over the mass news media network of the ceremonies, the full turn over of American jurisdiction to Iraq, or the declaration of the End of the Iraq War on January 1, 2009.

Chapter 4

~

Unique Analysis and De-mystifying Explanations from Insightful Observations

A Soldiers' Pay, an Explanation of the Natural Resource Credit

To help understand the concept of the natural resource credit it is first helpful to review how a soldier is paid in the United States. A soldier working for the military like anyone else working for the Government receives a paycheck from the Government which is payable by the United States Treasurer. Then the soldier has to calculate or pay someone to calculate his taxes, that is how much he has to pay back to the Government as income tax, which goes back to the United States Treasurer. The tax dollars go round full circle from the United States Treasurer to the military then back from the military to the United States Treasurer. Now it would seem more efficient if the military as well as all government employees were just paid the net difference to begin with and save all the paper, computations and cost of mailing. It is the same with the natural resource credit, the currency and monetary statutes would provide for the accounting of the extraction of natural gas, production of electricity, mining of minerals, and distribution services, and for crediting payment of consumer's electric bills (free electricity) and for full payment to the holders or the individual ownership interests of mineral/gas leases or such franchises as according to the fair capital value of the specific

American natural resources. The specific accounting and calculations needs further development and is beyond the scope of this book but not beyond the scope of CPA's, financiers, bankers and regulators. Such items as when the credit would be available, most likely it could "vest" at the age of eighteen years of age. It would not be transferable. Whether one would need to own real estate, like a home to in some way be a shareholder or stake-holder in America. Calculated as per the census perhaps. Again, I merely touch on these items here because the discussion is well beyond the scope of this book. Although the natural resource credit is more complex than the soldier pay example it is absolutely possible. If we fail to address this issue as a nation our society will either collapse or at best we will submit our general welfare and destiny to those who will govern us.

Oil & Water Economics

Oil and water are very similar once you get past the fact that one burns and the other puts out the fire. That is, the economics of oil and water are similar although their scientific properties are clearly different. Both are pumped out of the ground from wells and are processed before distribution to the consumer. Both oil and water are found in vast quantities underground. The extraction of oil and water from the ground are very similar in that the earth is drilled down to the water or oil, and then they are pumped out of the ground. Both need to be filtered, purified and spend time in reservoirs. Oil after coming up out of the ground requires distilling which means that the different compounds, the fuels, that is diesel, kerosene, gas and aviation fuel need to settle and separate out by resting undisturbed in a reservoir. Oil separates out by settling, the thick diesel fuel and kerosene goes to the bottom, vehicle fuel is more in the middle, and then the jet fuel is at the top. Additives such as detergents are added to produce a higher quality product. But the gas would burn in a motor without additives. The modern efficient distilling process is called fractional distillation where the crude oil is heated causing the range of compounds at different temperatures to boil out, that is to change to gases, producing separation, and then condensed back into liquids. In comparison, water is stored in reservoirs and chemicals are added to make the water fit for human consumption. Gas is distributed at the gasoline station pumps. Water is delivered to inside the consumers' home requiring a more extensive delivery system to the consumer. Wow what a difference in price. Vehicle gas ranges over $3.00 dollars per gallon. Nationally consumers use 400 gallons of water every day on an average. But water is so cheap per gallon that consumers only look at the gallons of use in the bill as $30.00 to $50.00 per month. Now it is clear that production is similar. Then why is there such an extreme variance in price to consumer? It is not the cost of transporting the petroleum from the Middle East or other far away places by oil tankers to the United States. Transporting the petroleum uses oil as fuel for the oil tanker's propulsion energy, fuel oil that was extracted, from the petroleum. Therefore, fuel oil is not an extra or additional expense. Also the marine diesel fuel used in the tankers is not otherwise a product sold in mass quantities in the United States. Clearly the main elements of cost include federal and state taxes, and of course oil company profits.

The "Long Distance Rip Off"

Once the Internet came out I realized that we were duped by the long distance charges, which were billed to the consumers by the telephone companies. Anyone can access Internet websites anywhere in the world without paying a long distance telephone charge. The telephone is similar to the Internet. An Internet user ramps up onto the Internet. The Internet is an energized system, a net, a web, which uses telephone wires, which many are the same as that the telephone companies use. It is the same with the telephone. The consumer plugs the telephone into the electric outlet and the telephone is energized. Everyone energizes his or her own telephone and the telephone system itself is energized. It does not cost anymore electric to call locally or to call out of state. You energize your phone. The system is energized by the telephone company. The person you are calling has his or her telephone energized. Are you getting it? Where does the extra cost come in to justify the extra charge for the long distance telephone call? No extra power is being put into the system because someone calls long distance. Remember how long the telephones have been around. Telephone companies started without computers. They lacked the technology to adjust the electricity of a large telephone net that would have depended on power requirements of every caller. The telephone companies had meters. The telephone companies placed meters in the wires at the state borders and other locations so that they can tag the calls for a long distance charge in order to bill you. Without the meters the calls would go through and no one know a long distance call went through to bill a long distance charge.

New Vehicles & New Riding Mowers

The average price in 2010 for a new motor vehicle was $28,000.00, approximately. The price of a new riding lawn mower varies from $1,000.00 to $5,000.00, approximately.

The engineering characteristics of motor vehicles and riding mowers do vary but are fundamentally very similar. The direct production costs, motors, metal and accessories are very similar due to the low cost of raw materials and wholesale mass purchasing. But the indirect costs of motor vehicle assembly vastly exceed that of lawn mower production because of labor union worker retirements and health care benefits, and motor vehicle production government regulations.

Riding lawn mowers are designed and produced to be operated on household lawns and turfs. Riding lawn mowers have engines, transmissions, blades and mechanisms to cut and propel the grass out from under the mower. Motor vehicle speeds exceed that of riding lawn mowers. Motor vehicles have larger engines and different transmissions than riding mowers. In production if the riding lawn motor was geared to run at high speeds, the cutting blade discarded, the interior expanded and more shiny, painted sheet metal added to the exterior, then the riding mower would be a car. The costs of the raw materials are similar for both. Scrap sheet metal is about $200.00 per ton. The majority of the price of a new vehicle is not in the production of the vehicle at all, but in non-production costs such as the cost of retirement and health care benefits of retired workers, OSHA, Environmental and array of multitudes of governmental regulations/compliance and of course CEO and upper level management compensation and bonuses.

Otherwise the sales price of motor vehicle would be a lot closer to that of a riding lawn mower.

All other consumer products have dropped in price since their entry into the consumer market, that is, all consumer products other than motor vehicles. VCR's (Beta-max) were $10,000.00 when they first went on the market in the early 1980's. Soon, they were down to $1,000.00. Then by the middle to late 1980's a VCR could be purchased for $400.00. When VCR's were getting replaced by DVD players in the late 1990's, early 2000, the sale price was $40.00. It was the same with computers. The first PC's were over $3,000.00 in the mid 1980's. As the prices dropped the technology improved multifold. The first computers had cathode ray picture tube monitors and required proficiency in typing line-by-line computer operating and software commands. Today's computers are screens with desktop icons to click on for word processing, spreadsheets and easy access to high speed Internet.

If the cost of all the other consumer products have dropped in value then the cost of motor vehicles should have dropped in value also. It is clear that big business interest and the government are artificially propping up the high prices of new motor vehicles. In order to assemble motor vehicles in the United States one needs to have a license issued by the federal government. There has only been a handful such licenses issued since the formation of government regulating agencies after the New Deal legislation of the 1930's. Prior to the licensing requirements many cities in the United States had small motor vehicle assemblage plants, which closed down because they could not obtain a license. Today if the federal license requirement was lifted and anyone could assemble motor vehicles, then the free market would dictate the price of the vehicles. Vehicle prices would then fall into line with the other consumer products pricing and spectacularly drop in price probably to an average price of $2,000.00 per car. Therefore lifting this regulation would immediately create jobs and at the same time provide relief to consumers who have been over paying for a consumer product for the last fifty (50) years.

Color Coding Of America

When I was a young child I first heard the term "Red Man" referring to American Indians. I looked at myself and I could see all the red in my face and arms. It never made any sense to me. Since then I have learned that skin color is determined by the type of and amount of melanin. Melanin is the pigment in the skin. There are two pigments for skin color in the human race. These pigments are known as melanin. The two types are the following: pheomelanin (red) and eumelanin (very dark brown). That is it. Then the skin color depends on the amount of each. If there is mostly red then the person is referred to as white. Mostly dark brown then the person is referred to as black. So you can consider the mixing of the red and dark brown as a continuum with one end as red called white and the other end dark brown called black with all the variations in between.

Ok, now can you see the nonsense? Where then on the continuum is the "Yellow Race" and the "Red Man." If you ever look at any government census reports you do not see these Yellow Race/Red Man color-coding categories being used. The old saying "divide and conquer" applies to ruling the people. Find reasons to divide the people and let them argue with each other so as to be preoccupied and miss the real issues, topics and concerns for the people.

Did the Jews kill Christ and the Church replace Israel?

Jesus and the twelve disciples were all Jews. If you were not a Jew then you were a Gentile. A Gentile just means a non-Jew, that is everyone else. But first let me clear up the term "Jew". The terms Israel, Israelites, Jacob, Hebrew, Jews and Zion are synonymous. Jacob was the "Father of Israel" because he was renamed Israel. Israel had twelve (12) sons. These 12 sons are the twelve (12) tribes of Israel. Israel or Israelites, therefore, is the name for the generations of people who are the descendants of Israel. Hebrew was the language of ancient Israel. Jew is short for Judah. Judah was the fourth son of Israel. Later Judah was the name of the southern kingdom of Israel. Zion is a mountain in Israel, where David conquered the inhabitants of the mountain then Jerusalem was built on this Mount Zion. Mt Zion is symbolic for the whole nation of Israel.

Jesus came to the "lost children of Israel." In the Gospel of Matthew, Matthew 15:24, it is recorded that Jesus replied to a Canaanite woman "I was sent only to the lost sheep of Israel." Jesus came first to the Jews. He came as their expected Messiah. He came to preach the gospel Himself to the Jews only. Afterwards it was preached to the Gentiles, but the ministry of Jesus was confined almost entirely to the Jews.

In Matthew 23:37, Jesus was unable to reach the lost children of Israel: "O Jerusalem, Jerusalem, you who kill the prophets and stone those sent to you, how often I have longed to gather your children together, as a hen gathers her chicks under her wings, but you were not willing." Also "Salvation" up and through the time of Jesus was only for the Jews. The Jews were the chosen people of the Lord. It was not until after Jesus resurrected that salvation was opened up to all who accepted Jesus as their savior. In John

4:21 Jesus answered a Samaritan woman who had stated that the Jews claim that the place where one must worship was in Jerusalem: "Believe me, woman, a time is coming when you will worship the Father neither on this mountain nor in Jerusalem. You Samaritans worship what you do not know; we worship what we do know, for salvation is from the Jews. Yet a time is coming and has now come when the true worshipers will worship the Father in spirit and truth, for they are the kind of worshipers the Father seeks. God is spirit, and his worshipers must worship in spirit and in truth." Then in Mathew 28:18, known as The Great Commission the resurrected Jesus opened salvation up to all the world: "All authority in heaven and on earth has been given to me. Therefore go and make disciples of all nations, baptizing them in the name of the Father and of the Son and of the Holy Spirit, and teaching them to obey everything I have commanded you. And surely I am with you always, to the very end of the age."

Apostle Paul makes it clear that Jews would be saved. "And so all Israel will be saved, as it is written: The deliverer will come from Zion; he will turn godlessness away from Jacob. And this is my covenant with them when I take away their sins." Romans 11 26:27. Therefore, no matter how you want to interpret "all Israel will be saved" you have to understand that at least a number of Jews can be saved.

Next many think that the Church replaced the role of the Jews and that the Jews were cast out by the Lord. That is just not so. Apostle Paul explains in the metaphor of the olive tree and branches and the Lord cut off a branch from the Olive tree and grafted in a wild olive branch. The Olive tree is Israel. The wild olive branch is the Gentiles. It is also to one's benefit to heed Apostle Paul's warning: "… do not boast over those branches. If you do, consider this: You do not support the root, but the root supports you. You will say then, "Branches were broken off so that I could be grafted in." Granted. But they were broken off

70

because of unbelief, and you stand by faith. Do not be arrogant, but be afraid. For if God did not spare the natural branches, he will not spare you. Romans 11 15:17

Chapter 5

~

You Need an Outline:
We have a genuine Judeo/Christian
History

This book is of maximum importance because our society is
fundamentally changing and otherwise our way of life is going to
be radically different and if we know the beginnings of our society,
western civilization, then we can better prepare ourselves for what
is coming. And, maybe we can help steer it for the better. We
need to draw on creative ways to respond and restore America.

An outline provides a rough draft, a map of the landscape, and a
broad view that allows one to connect the dots and fill-ins with the
theories and the facts. Where our society is headed is produced
from independent thought that analyzes and tests all names and
facts. For example, if you are reading this book you may have
gone to "public" school, which I prefer to use the term
"government" school. God Bless all our teachers who care about
our children and are educating them. There are two types of
schools, schools that are operated by the government called public
schools and schools operated by individuals called "private
schools." Labeling or name-calling is powerful. These names are
misleading and should be discarded. The labeling of the names
public and private cast a false negative inference on schools. Both
government and private schools are open to the public.
Admissions, enrollment, policies and activities for both are public.

One school is operated by the government and funded by taxes. The other school is operated by individuals for profit and is funded by tuition. Government schools cost $14,000 to $18,000 per student. Schools operated by individuals cost $3,000 to $4,000 per student and the students learn more! Also with taxes you never quit paying, whereas tuition ends with graduation.

Endorse the revival and returning to our Christian, political and historical truths and this book is my contribution, which is presented as an outline of what you need to know. Martin Luther in the Middle Ages made known that the church was wrong about indulgences. Indulgences means forgiveness of sins by paying money to the church or performing a deed. The Pope, Bishop or Church authority gave indulgences. In other words an indulgence is purchasing a pardon for one's sins. Martin Luther, around October 31, 1517, provided clear evidence that the widespread practice of granting indulgences by the church was not Biblical in his famous "Disputation of Martin Luther on the Power and Efficacy of Indulgences", which came to be known as "The 95 Theses", which changed Western Society and saved multitudes of lives. In 1775 the two lanterns were hung indicating the British were coming by sea, Paul Revere rode off to warn Samuel Adams and John Hancock that British troops were marching to arrest them, otherwise the American Revolution and democracy would have been cut down, stopped before the Colonist would have ever had a chance to begin, originate and organize our beliefs into our founding political documents and form our democracy.

Again today men and women are providing news, messages, networks and copies of accurate past American and Western History, Christian beliefs and present-day information and current events.

A Brief Summary of
The Beginnings of Western
Civilization

Biblical Creation: Approximately 10,000 years ago (sources vary). Adam and Eve is the beginning of civilization as found in Genesis. Mitochondria DNA is passed from mother to daughter. Unlike the Y chromosome, both males and females get their mother's mitochondria, though the males do not pass it. The initial mitochondrial DNA imprinted in the first woman's cells has divided and replicated themselves in generation after generation since the first woman's time on Earth. Clearly today's science supports that Eve was the grandparent to us all. If as science teaches us that this mitochondrial DNA passed down from one woman to the next, then why not that woman be the Biblical Eve?

And as the Biblical Eve then her world was destroyed in Noah's Flood. Then geography as we know it was restructured from the flood. After the Flood, the world was left totally reshaped from the Earth being covered with water and undercurrents of tsunamis. Noah and his three sons and families departed the arc at Mount Ararat in Eastern Turkey. The first city Noah and his descendants populated was Chorenensis (ancient Hebrew name), also known as Idsheuan (ancient Armenian name) situated in Eastern Turkey (formerly Armenia) near the departure site from the arc, which is near the border of Iraq. They migrated approximately 400 miles from Eastern Turkey to the plain of Shinar (formerly known as Sumer, also known as Mesopotamia) and now known as modern day Iraq. Turkey borders Iraq. Noah and his descendents were the only people left alive on planet Earth. All the peoples of the world, clans, tribes and extended families are descendants of Noah, Noah's three sons and their wives.

Historical supportive evidence that Noah's family colonized the globe is found in the recorded history of the world in Judeo/Christian and non-Judeo/Christian records. For example, the writings of Josephus, a first century Jewish diplomat, general (military commander), and historian, which are still preserved and readily available to read today, references extensive accounts of Noah's Flood documented in accepted academic texts of his time such as Nicolaus of Damascus, a friend and a bibliographer author of Herod the Great, who wrote the *Universal History* in 144 books, now only fragments remain. Also in writings of other historians such as Berosus, who wrote on the history of Babylon and Maneho who wrote on the history of Egypt (books lost).

Noah's Flood: Approximately 10,000 years ago (sources vary). As indicated in Genesis 10: 32, all peoples (ancient and modern) are all derived from Noah's three sons, Shem, Ham, and Japheth. Typically referred to as the "Table of Nations." There is an entire science, Genealogy of Mankind, the Origin of Races tracing all the peoples of the world from Noah's three sons. The Jews trace their ancestry back through Shem. Noah--> Shem--> Eber--> Terah --> Abraham (birth name Abram) --> Issac --> Jacob (renamed Israel) --> Israelites, modern-day Jews. After landing on Mount Ararat, the highest summit of Europe, now known as Turkey, the descendants of Noah kept together at first, then broke up into small groups (a number of extended families) and eventually arrived in Mesopotamia (modern day Iraq), approximately 400 miles from Mount Ararat.

There is a plethora of scientific evidence supporting creation and a world flood. Multitudes of cultures such as the Aztecs of Mexico and the Miao People of China separated by continents and oceans have accounts of creation and world flood. The geological evidence is right in front of our eyes. From an airplane's eye view one can see how the receding, draining waters formed the Grand Canyon and the network of other great canyons throughout the

American southwest, and how the lengthy tectonic plates suddenly rupturing, pushing up, heaping up molten material from the deep like conveyor belts to form the present-day continuous mountain ridges. Biblically described as "springs of the great deep burst forth, and the floodgates of the heavens were opened" Genesis 7:11. The successive tsunami tidal currents, swells and waves moving through the deep waters sculptured the cooling molten material. Do not write off Biblical creation and Noah's flood. It is true.

Mesopotamia: Approximately 10,000 years ago (sources vary). Mesopotamia also known as land between two rivers, are namely the Tigris River and the Euphrates River. The descendants of Noah following departure from the Arc traveled together at first, then divided into small groups and numbers of descendants of Noah eventually populated Mesopotamia. Mesopotamia today is essentially **Iraq**. Mesopotamia consisted of diverse largely independent city-states with their own cultures, completely different religions, languages, and kings. History is said to start in Mesopotamia by secular scholars only because there are records of civilizations found there other than Biblical or records from any of the whole body of Jewish law and teachings. Such secular records found were Sumerian records.

Sumer: The Sumerians (former inhabitants of modern day Iraq) were descendents of Noah who strayed from the Lord. The Sumerians differed from the decedents of Abraham in that they believed in multitudes of gods and committed human sacrifice. Sumerian cuneiform pictograph type writings of canals, dikes, and reservoirs, indicated that the Sumerian were farmers who perfected irrigation agriculture and waged war and so forth. Otherwise Sumerian writings do not assist in any way to clarify the culture, beliefs or shared values of the peoples of their society. Read for yourself the translations of Sumerian writings now available on the Internet. One of the highly regarded Sumerian writings is

"Enmerkar and the Lord of Aratta". Enmerkar simply is an interchange of threats between city-state rulers, which include references to Sumerian deities and other deities. The reference to Gods and Goddess are claims and assertions that the Deity favors the one kingdom ruler over the other kingdom's ruler so he can extort contributions from the other ruler, it's only intending to intimidate the other ruler. It goes back and forth. It does not appear that either ruler is much persuaded because at one point the messenger is not sent back for after five years to ten years, that is to the one ruler "splits the reed with an axe".

Ruthless rulers who sacrifice constituents to deities are tyrants who rule by terror. Eventually over time the Sumerian city-states were formed into an empire and successive empires. These empires also referred to as dynasties were eventually overcome by the Babylonians and the Sumerian identity is lost. There is no basis to give these secular records any more credibility than the ancient Hebrew records. Quite the contrary, ancient Hebrew teachings and writings are inspirational and enlightening in moral, intellectual, and spiritual improvement, such as found in Ecclesiastes 3: "To everything there is a season, and a time to every purpose under the heaven." Also there is undeniably dedication to preserving and duplicating scrolls throughout Jewish antiquity and thereafter through Christian monks. Additionally there are no independent sources to explain known inaccuracies in chronology and inconsistencies of Sumerian records.

The Sumerians built Ziggurats, stepped heathen structures. The Greatest of them – the Sumerian Ziggurat of Ur. Today in modern day Iraq approximately 40 miles from Baghdad stands in what was known in the ancient world as Ur, in the ancient capital of Sumeria, the ruins of Ur's ziggurat, a massive solid stepped tower, surrounded by a cemetery which contains the tombs of ancient Sumerian rulers. You can go visit it by signing up for a tour. Just remember human beings were sacrificed in the ziggurat. The Bible in Genesis 11:2 indicates that the Tower of Babel was in the plain of Shinar. Shinar is an ancient name for modern-day Iraq, same place. The Bible does not record the destruction of the Tower of Babel but other sources do such as Josephus, "God overturns the tower with a great wind." Josephus (Antiquities 1.4.3). There you have just been presented with archeological evidence, Biblical Scriptural evidence, and non-Biblical evidence of the Tower of Babel.

Israel also finds its roots in Ur of the Chaldeans (now Northern Iraq). The majority of scholars conclude that Abraham (birth name Abram) son of Terah was a descendant of the peoples from Ur of the Chaldeans (now Northern Iraq). "Terah took his son Abram, his grandson Lot son of Haran, and his daughter-in-law Sarai, the wife of his son Abram, and together they set out from Ur of the Chaldeans to go to Canaan." Genesis 11:31. Canaan is the historical name of what today correspondingly is the region encompassing modern-day Israel.

Israel: **Ancient Israel**, Abraham was fourth generation after Noah. Noah--> Shem--> Eber--> Terah --> Abraham. Abraham on his way to Egypt traveled through Negev (Negev desert region in southern Israel is approximately half of Israel's land today). Abraham left the land of his birth, Ur of the Chaldeans, which is the same as the plain of Shinar (modern-day Iraq). Genesis 11:28. Then Abraham traveled to Canaan (Israel), whereupon the Lord gave Abraham the title deed to Israel. Genesis 12:7. Approximate 500 years later, Joshua defeated 31 Canaanite Kings. The Lord gave Israel all the land sworn to Abraham and the Israelites took possession of the land and settled there. Joshua 21: 43-45.

Israel: **The Golden Age**. King David then his son Solomon ruled Israel from 990 BC to 928 BC. David enlarged the kingdom and fought numerous adversaries. Solomon reigned during Israel's peak political and military power. Solomon "ruled over all the kingdoms west of the Euphrates River from Tiphsah to Gaza; he was at peace with all his neighbors." I Kings, 4:24. Israel invented the "Bessemer Process" of refining steel in a large blast furnace during the Golden Age. Evidence is found in the remains of the smelting facilities at Ezion-Geber (southern Israel). Ezion-Geber was the "Pittsburgh" of ancient Israel. After Joshua there are no accounts of battles with the Phoenicians. Evidence supports that there must have been a working treaty between the Phoenicians and Israelis which provided the seaboard freight shipping of items for King Solomon's magnificent temple and most extensive zoo with animals and birds from all around the world.

   Unfortunately after Solomon his son Rehoboam was not able to keep the Israel Kingdom together. The kingdom divided into two kingdoms. The northern ten tribes became the nation of Israel. The Capital was Samaria. The southern two tribes became the nation of Judah. The capital was Jerusalem. The name Jew came from inhabitant of Judah. For approximately 200 years Israel and Judah were ruled by kings who followed foreign gods like Bael and brought destruction on themselves by losing the Lord's Blessings.

Phoenicia: The Phoenicians lived in city-states among the Israelis in which today is modern Israel and Lebanon. Phoenicians roots are also traced back to the city-states of Mesopotamia and ancestry through Ham, son of Noah. The Phoenicians were also known during the ancient time as Sidonians. Named for inhabitants of the city of Sidon, now known as Tyre in Lebanon. Tyre, a seaport city was the most famous Phoenician city, was referred to in the Bible, the notorious "Jezebel, wife of King Ahab, was the daughter of Ethbaal, King of Tyre and Sidon." 1 Kings 16:31. "So give orders that cedars of Lebanon be cut for me. My men will work with yours, and I will pay you for your men whatever wages you set. You know that we have no one so skilled in felling timber as the Sidonians." 1 Kings 5:6. The Phoenicians were the great mariners, in their ships made of cedar from Lebanon sailed in the ancient Mediterranean, southwestern European ports and northern Africa. There is evidence to support that during the Diaspora (Diaspora the term for forced expulsions of the Israelites from what is now the states of Israel, Jordan and parts of Lebanon) that the Phoenicians took the Israelites to America. These Israelites are called the lost tribes of Israel. The Mormons (Church of Jesus Christ of Latter-Day Saints) believe according to Joseph Smith in his Book of Mormons that one of these Israeli tribes, the Manasseth came to America. It is part of their faith. There is evidence such as Indian grave markers, which are actually written in ancient Hebrew, Cherokee Indians have a "Day of Atonement" and the ancient copper mine workings around the northern shores of Lake Superior.

Also the first alphabet, the Phoenician alphabet, was similar or a dialect of ancient Hebrew and or Aramic. The word "Aramaic" comes from the biblical Aram (pronounced AH-rahm), son of Shem and grandson of Noah. Aram was the father of the ancient civilization of the Aramaic speaking Arameans. The area is now known as Syria. The Aramaic language was spoken by Abraham, Moses and Jesus Christ. Some of the Bible was written in Aramaic. After the coming of Jesus Christ, the Arameans of Aram-Naharaim accepted the teachings of Christ and formed the Syrian Church of Antioch, where, for the first time, the followers of Jesus Christ were called "Christians" (Acts 11:26). The Arameans underwent a name change after conversion to Christianity to "Syrians" to be set them apart from the Arameans, who were not converted.

Egypt: Egypt the land of Ancient Egyptians tombs, mummies, mystic gods, pyramids, the sphinx, hieroglyphics, King Tut and the Pharaohs. Moses led the Hebrew nation out of Egypt. Egypt is one of the most frequently mentioned names in the Bible. The Bible frequently uses the common Hebrew name for Egypt, which

is Mizraim. The first non-Hebrew known name for Egypt was Hi-
ku-ptah, which is believed to mean "Place of the Spirit of the god
Ptah." This name Hi-ku-ptah was Hellenized by the Greeks,
transforming it into Ai-gu-ptos, which in Latin became Aegyptus,
and then later in English modern day is Egypt.

The Egyptians are descendants of Ham. Noah--> Ham -->
Mizarim. Genesis 10:6. Mizarim was second generation after
Noah. Mizraim, the Hebrew name for Egypt, was the name of one
of the sons of Ham. Mizraim translates as the "Land of Mizraim."
Of the sons of Ham, Canaan, Mizraim, Cush, and Phut started out
traveling together. The descendents of Canaan inhabited Canaan.
Mizrraim stayed in Egypt. Cush settled in Ethiopia. And, Phut
settled in Libya. Phut is the Hebrew name for Libya. There is
evidence to support that many family groups, descendents of the
sons of Ham migrated to Oklahoma, Texas, New Mexico and
eventually Mexico, establishing the forceful Aztec tribes with their
sinister, fortified cities. Did you ever wonder why the pyramids in
South America looked like the pyramids in Egypt? The answer is
that the South American pyramids were built by the relatives of the
people who built them in Egypt.

The Persians conquered Egypt in 525 BC lead by the Persian king
Cambyses. The Persians ruled Egypt until when Alexander the
Great invaded Egypt and established the Ptolemaic dynasty 332
BC – 30 BC. After his takeover, Alexander was accepted as the
new pharaoh, and he established the flourishing city of Alexandria,
which became as well known as its founder, particularly for the
historic Grand Library of over a half a million documents
maintained by the ancient Hebrews that once stood there. Next,
Augustus annexed Egypt as a province of the Roman Empire and
Egypt was ruled by the Romans until 642 A.D. During the Roman
occupancy, Christianity came to Egypt. The Egyptian branch of the
Christian church, known as Coptic, is one of the oldest in the
world, and is still there today. The Moslim Conquest 642 A.D.,

whereupon, Egypt was conquered by the Muslims. When the Muslims conquered Alexandria, most of the population evacuated the city. The vacant houses were occupied by the Muslims. There is no longer a Grand Library in Alexandria, it was destroyed. Many believe the books were destroyed under the Roman Occupation others contend that the books were destroyed by the conquering Muslims using the books as tinder for the bathhouses of the city. The Muslims built a new capital, founded at Fustat. Fustat later was absorbed into the present day Egypt capital Cairo.

Of the over 80 Million living in Egypt today over half are peasant farmers whose lifestyle has changed little since the Muslim conquest of 642 A.D. Islam is the country's official religion. Television is state-owned and sets the tone for daily programming. The country's primary source of income is revenue from exporting oil. Many average Egyptians are living in poverty and are subsidized by the government. While the population continues to rise rapidly it is not clear that economic issues will be addressed. Terrorism is on the rise against Christians and Western Civilization. The Alexandria bombing, an attack on Christians was carried out early New Year's Day 2011, in the Egyptian city of Alexandria. At least 23 people died in the attack, all of them Christians. About 97 other Christians were injured. This violence continues to escalate against Egypt's Christian minority (still known as Coptic Christians), since the Kosheh massacre in 2000, which left 21 Christians dead.

Assyria: Assyria a relatively short lived Empire. Assyria was the result of ancient conquests rising out of the city-state, Ashur, Assyria translated was the Land of Ashur. Ashur was also the name of the chief god of the Assyrians. The Assyrian Empire's capital was Nineveh. Both Ashur and Nineveh were located near the modern day city of Mosul in Iraq. The Assyrian Empire conquered the northern kingdom of Israel. The Assyrians tortured, decapitated and forced many Israelites into slavery resulting in the

Lost Ten Tribes of Israel. Nineveh was attacked and destroyed by the Babylonians. The conquest was ruthless and devastating. The Assyrian Empire fell, and the fall was hard. Nahum in the Bible, Nahum 3, prophesied prior to the destruction of Nineveh that Nineveh would be destroyed and would never recover because of their cruel treatment of the Israelites and other people. As we can see today, Nahum was right Nineveh never recovered.

Babylon: Babylon means "babilu" (gate of god). Babylon defeated Judea, the Southern Kingdom, plundered Jerusalem, hauled Jews off into slavery and destroyed Solomon's temple. Prior to the occupation many Jews traveled to North Africa, Asia Minor, Europe and possibly North America. This dispersion of the Jews is called the "Disapora." Babylon was the City-State that through conquest grew into the Babylon Empire. Babylon became the capital of the Babylon Empire. Babylon Empire was Mesopotamia/Sumerians conquered and is modern day Iraq. Babylon the ancient city in the plain of shinar (Babylon) on the Euphrates River, was 50 miles, approximately south of modern-day Baghdad. Babylon was founded by Nimrod (Genesis 10). Nimrod fourth generation after Noah, Noah--> Ham --> Cush --> Nimrod. Nimrod is credited with building the Tower of Babel, a ziggurat described structure. Above, in the section on Sumerians, I described the ziggurats, which were built by the Sumerians, which were stepped heathen structures. The Bible in Genesis indicates that the Tower of Babel was blasphemy, which God condemned (Gen. 11). After the destruction of the Tower of Babel, Babylon remained.

   Hammurabi was the first ruler of Babylon. Kassite tribes, a people who were living in Mesopotamia over took the city of Babylon. The Kassite kings then ruled Babylon. But Kassite kings and people soon were absorbed and lost into the Babylonian debauchery culture and heathen beliefs as follows: The mystic egg of Babylon fell from heaven into the Euphrates River. Hatched from the egg was Venus Ishtar. Ishtar was the Goddess of love and fertility. At Ishtar Festivals the Babylonians would have sexual orgies in the name of Ishtar. At the temple women were treated as being worshiped, as if they were Ishtar. They did not worship Ishtar or any gods. Women sacrificed their virginity at the Ishtar Festivals or became temple prostitutes. Centuries later the Roman Emperor Constantine who gave Christianity legal status in the Roman Empire changed the celebration of the Resurrection of Jesus Christ from the Passover date to resemble this pagan date and holiday consequently mixing it into the Resurrection of Jesus.

Nebuchadnezzar ruled Babylon for 45 years. Interesting facts about Nebuchadnezzar and Babylon according to the historian Herodotus:

- Nebuchadnezzar conquered Egypt.

- The Euphrates River flowed through the middle of the enormously walled city. Drawbridges were closed at night.

- Water was raised from the river by hydraulic pumps.

- Golden image of Baal and the Golden Table (Weight over 50,000 lbs of solid gold.)

- 2 golden lions, a solid gold human figure (18 feet high)

In 539 B.C. Cyrus led the Persian army into victory over the Babylonians' city, which was protected by enormous walls, and was built on either side of the Euphrates River. Since Babylon could not possibly be taken by assault, Cyrus channeled the Euphrates River away from the city, and when the river lowered, his army marched up through the dry riverbed during a Feast and took the city. Nothing remains of Babylon today except a series of widely scattered mounds. The Kassite peoples migrated into central Europe where they were called "German" or "Germanni," a general name later used by the Romans to represent all Assyrian tribes.

Persia: Modern day Iran. Cyrus, a Persian king after military conquest merged the two groups of people the Persians (descendents of Shem) and the Medes (descendents of Japheth) who were living in what is now known as modern day Iraq into one empire. Cyrus is known for skillfully having ruled the people he conquered by appointing Median as well as Persian officials and allowing the conquered people to speak their own language, practice their own religion, and follow their own ways of life. Cyrus wanted to conquer the whole world and he wanted it for religious reasons. Cyrus believed the teachings of Zoroaster. The teachings of Zoroaster paralleled the teachings of Judaism. The Creation account and Flood account are very similar. According to Genesis record of Creation humanity is descended from a single couple, Adam and Eve, Zoraster taught the same, their names were Mashya (man) and Mashyana (women).

  After conquering Babylon, Cyrus received from his Babylon predecessor Judah. Cyrus allowed the Jews to return to their homeland, and he allowed Governor Nehemiah of Jerusalem to rebuild the temple and walls of Jerusalem and Ezra to restore Jewish religious life in Judah. Years later when United States recognized Israel as an independent state in 1948, President Truman said: "I am Cyrus." In 336 B.C. Alexander the Great the king of Macedonia defeated Persians.

The Greek Empire: Known in ancient days as Macedonia. Macedonia took its name from the mythical Macedon the son of Zeus. Alexander the Great was born in Pella. Pella was the ancient capital of Macedonia, ransacked later by the Romans, and then further destroyed by an earthquake. Ruins/remains are visible at modern-day, Pella Greece. The Greek Empire was a collection of City-States into Empires and former/earlier empires. The Empire included the Minoan Civilization and well-known city-states Athens, Sparta and Corinth. And, Greeks were also called Mycenaens after the large city of Mycenae. The Mycenaens destroyed Knossos in Crete, and took control of the eastern part of the Mediterranean. Alexander the Great defeated the Persian Empire at the Battle of Gaugamela, which took place near present day Mosul, Iraq. Alexander increased the Greek Empire all the way from Egypt to India. Greece remained a world power until 150 B.C. when it was conquered by Rome.

The contributions to Western Civilization are numerous: Architecture, painting, sculpture, columns, art, literary sources, epic poems, Iliad and Odyssey, Homer, math, science, and theater, Hippocratic Oath, Democracy, Greek Philosophers: Aristotle, Socrates.

Greek Mythology ended up being troubling for the empire. The source of Greek mythology is traced to earlier inhabitants of the Balkan Peninsula, now present day Bulgaria and Serbia. These earlier inhabitants of the Balkan Peninsula came up with Animism. Animism is the idea that spirits not only exist in humans but also in animals, plants, rocks, and natural phenomena such as lightning and thunder. Eventually, these vague spirits were given human names, their status as spirits were elevated to gods, and stories of powers, conquest, battles, heroism and adventure were fabricated about them.

Alexander the Great built Alexandria in Egypt, which became the capital of the Macedonia Empire (known today as the Greek Empire). Hellas was the Jewish community in Alexandria. Hellas was the largest Jewish community in the ancient world. The name of the city, Hellas is the source of the term Hellenic. Hellenic means relating to or characteristic of the classical Greek civilization. Due to the Hellenic effect on the Jews it became necessary to translate the Hebrew Scriptures from Hebrew to Greek, which resulted in the **Septuagint**. The Septuagint in Latin means Seventy, which is the nearest round number for Seventy-Two translations. Six Jews from each of the twelve tribes of Israel independently translated the Hebrew texts into Greek, and there was not one discrepancy among the Seventy-Two translations. Hence it was named the Septuagint.

After King Alexander died the Kingdom was divided. Ptolemy became ruler of Egypt and Israel with the capital in Alexandria. Seleucus became ruler of Syria and Babylon with the capital at Antioch. The Ptolemies and the Seleucids battled it out. The Seleucids won. King Antiochus, took the title Epiphanies, meaning "God Manifest" then determined to stamp out Judaism banned sacrifices at the temple, the observance of the Sabbath, teaching the Scriptures, and circumcism backed up with the penalty of death. The Jewish **Maccabean Revolt** over through the Seleucids and self-ruled for approximately one hundred years. Pompey marched into Jerusalem in 63 B.C., and Israel again became subject to rule by a foreign empire.

The Roman Empire: 753 B.C through 476 A.D. The Roman Empire lasted over 1,200 years. Most significant to Western Civilization was the birth and Resurrection of Jesus Christ, the early Church, Constantine giving Christianity legal status in the Empire, but mixing it with Babylon Ishtar, democracy, architect, arch, dome, Latin, and numerous other contributions.

Rome fell with the greatest military at its disposal, the Roman Legion and a police force rivaled by none. Its cities were sacked and looted by the Visigoths. Visigoths were the German nomads who had migrated to central Europe from prior other empires like the Kassite from the Babylon Empire. The Roman leadership was so corrupt, decadent, and immoral and known for excessive self-indulgence, sexual perversions and debauchery that the citizens, the military the administrators simply could not stomach to obey them. So they did little to defend themselves.

Arabian Christian History, Pre-Islam in Arabian Peninsula, 167 B.C. to Present: The Jews, Zoroastrians and Christians taught one true God centuries before Mohammed. The southern end of the Arabian Peninsula, today, known as Yemen, had been ruled by the Jews from the time of the Jewish Maccabaens to Herod in Judea. Christianity followed into the Arabian Peninsula and was wide spread, also Zoroastrianism was present in the peninsula. Christianity was established in Egypt, Syria and Arabia for many centuries before Islam. The Nestorian Christians from Syria are credited with establishing the Christian community at Najran. Najran is a city in southwestern Saudi Arabia near the border of Yemen. The Christian Syrian name for God is Alaha, derived from the Hebrew Elohim, resembles the Islamic name of God, Allah. Christian Arabs since ancient time through present time use the name Allah for God, even to this day.

Islam: Rise and Fall of political Islam. The religion of Islam teaches: " there is no God but Allah and Muhammad is the messenger of Allah,..." Christians really do not know the basics of the Christianity faith. Numbers of Christians do not even know that Jesus was a Jew. Most likely many followers of Islam lack knowledge of the basic beliefs of Islam. Do Muslims know that the individuals referred to in the Qur'an such as Adam, Noah, Jesus and Moses are the same individuals in the Torah (except for Jesus) and all are in the Bible?

Political Islam is not about religious Islam. Political Islam also does not discuss or examine the aspects of Islamic jurisprudence and scholastic content. Political Islam is a general heading referring to the movement, which sees Islam as the main vehicle for restructuring of the ruling class, creating new societies and world domination. As such, it opposes, confronts and triumphs over western society, especially the capitalist world, to overcome it and exchange its share of power and influence in the world order.

Mohammed was born 570, A.D., in Mecca into the Koreish (Quraish) family, a family of recent arrival to Mecca, one of the ten dominant Bedouin families in Saudi Arabia at the time. Many texts refer to these Bedouin families as tribes or clans. Bedouin, defined means the families, which were nomadic desert-dwelling peoples of predominantly Arab descent, which would include descendents of Abraham. Noah--> Shem--> Eber--> Terah --> Abraham (birth name Abram) --> Issac/Ishmeal --> Arabs, + --> Moab/ Esau --> Arabs.

Mohammed's father, died before or shortly after Mohammed's birth. At six years of age he lost his mother. Then two years later his grandfather died. Thereafter, Abu Talib, his uncle tended to him. Muhammad, according to Muslim theologists, did not receive any education, and at a young age started working with the caravans. During caravan travels at the age of twelve a Syrian Christian Monk first affected Mohammed with the idea of one God. In his 25th year Mohammed was employed (commissioned sales) by Chadidja (also Khadidja), a rich Koreish widow and he worked for her caravans at the fairs, whom he married although she was much older (at least 40 years old) and twice widowed. She bore him 7 children. Chadidja died when Mohammed was 49 years of age. All their children predeceased him except his daughter, Fatimah. After Chadidja died Mohammed married nine or ten more wives. Western historians have been less than kind reporting one of the marriages, the marriage of Mohammed to Aisha. Aisha was six years old when engaged to Muhammad. Records vary as to her age as nine or ten, and more recently reported as fourteen or fifteen years at the time of marriage, when the marriage was consummated in Medina.

Mohammed was 40 years of age when it is said he received his first divine communication in the cave of the Hira Mountain, near Mecca. Mohammed proclaimed Allah as the one true god and rejected the idol worship of Mecca. The Koreish were the dominant tribe in Mecca, the city was ruled by Koreish men who had grown wealthy from the success of their caravan ventures. At the time of Muhammad the Koreish family, his extended family were in charge of the Kaaba. The Kaaba building, houses the black Kaaba stone. The Kaaba building is the sacred shrine of Mecca and had been there long before the Koreish family had arrived in Mecca. The Kaaba is a cube-shaped building in Mecca, Saudi Arabia. The significant feature of the Kaaba is the Black Stone, believed by Muslims to be placed there by Abraham and Ishmael. Most Western historian sources indicate that the Black Stone was placed there by the pre-Islamic pagan cultures of Arabia. This term "pre-Islamic pagan cultures" is Western terminology synonymous for Bedouin families before Mohammed's time who were not Jews or Christians.

Such Bedouin families each had its particular deity represented there at the Kaaba and other religious figures were there, including Jesus and Mary. Some accounts state there was an idol for every day of the year. All these idols and figures were a way of harmony, sharing and respect for all to participate in social events. Mohammed encountered hostility from his extended Koreish family by claiming the shrine for only one God of the new religion of Islam that he preached. He wanted the Kaaba to be dedicated to the worship of the one God alone, and all pagan idols, Jew and Christian statues evicted. Mohammed's family, the Koreish family persecuted and harassed him continuously because advocating casting out all the other idols and statues of all the other families was vehemently opposed by the other Bedouin families, creating a enormous societal upheaval which obviously was not good for business. Mohammed's wife and uncle, members of Mohammed's immediate family hid him to protect him. Chadidja, his wife died in 619 A.D. His uncle Abu Talib, died a year later in 620 A.D. Opposition to Mohammed and his followers was so fierce, and protection of his close family members gone, Mohammed and his follower had to escape to Medina in 622. Escaping to Medana is called "The Hijira."

Mohammed stayed in Medina for about fifteen years. The Arabs being aware that the Jews were still looking for the Messiah wanted to find the Messiah first, and in an effort to settle a territorial dispute between the Jews and the Arabs, the Arabs presented Mohammed to the Jews. The Jewish families rejected his claims as a prophet and ridiculed his revelations. The Jews were aware that Mohammed's family had hid him or he would have been killed. Mohammed had no ministry like other prophets or Jesus Christ, no healing the sick, performing miracles and teaching the multitudes. The Jews and the Christians to this day have never accepted Mohammed as a prophet. The battles continued between the Muslims in Medina and the Jews in Mecca. Mohammed married nine or ten more women. These marriages helped Mohammed form political alliances. Mohammed's followers increased in numbers. Other families entered into agreements with Mohammed, and in 628 A.D., an agreement allowed Mohammed and his followers to enter Mecca. In 630 A.D. Mohammed managed to take control over Mecca without any resistance. A general amnesty was granted to all of Mohammed's Koreish family, even persecutors of Mohammed, and even if they did not convert to Islam. The Muslims robbed caravans heading toward Mecca to raise money for military conquest. This is where the Muslim doctrine of "Jihad" was first created. Then from Mecca, the Muslims waged Jihad on the surrounding cities forcing them to accept Islam as their religion and Mohammed as their prophet. In the year 621, at the age of 51 years old, Mohammed died.

Mohammed's death in Islam is known as Mohammed's Ascension. He flew on the magical Winged-Horse of Fire which is named Burak, meaning "White Horse but seen as "Thunder-Lightning." Mohammed's Ascension is known as "Miraj" or "Stairway to Heaven" began when Mohammed went to sleep on a carpet "Magic Carpet Ride".

At the time of his death, Mohammed had conquered all the Bedouin, Jewish and Christian families of Arabia and the Empire extended throughout the Arabian Peninsula.

Islamic Conquest after Mohammed: After the death of Mohammed was a century of fierce internal conflicts, divisions and multiple murderous struggles, following the murder of a caliph (Islam leader) a new caliph would emerge, and rapid military conquest and expansion of the Muslim Empire. The Muslim Empire expansion stretched from Pakistan across Asia, Iran, Armenia, Iraq, Syria, Israel, Egypt, North Africa, Libya, Tunisia, Algeria, Morocco, Sicily, Cyprus, Portugal, Spain, to the borders of France.

The fall of Constantinople, 1453: The atrocities and carnage during the victory are recorded and described in detail by eyewitnesses. Muslim soldiers massacred one and a half million inhabitants. Muslim soldiers smashed into private homes and looted. Shops in the city markets were looted. Churches, Monasteries and Convents, Holy places were decimated and destroyed. Inhabitants were killed, nuns were raped, worshippers slaughtered and many city inhabitants committed suicide to save themselves from torment. Muslim soldiers killed, raped young boys and young women, looting, and burning went on and on for days. The splendid, beautiful Christian Holy buildings were looted, artworks destroyed, precious manuscripts were burnt and lost forever. Thousands of inhabitants were taken into slavery.

Nobility, Christians, Jews, Zoroastrians none were spared all were treated with equal ruthlessness.

The Muslim empire reached its furthest expansion. In 732 A.D., the advancing Muslims were stopped at the Battle of Tours by the French General Charles Martel, which ended any further northward Muslim advancement out of Muslim controlled Spain. The Battle of Covadonga in the summer of 722 A.D. was the first major victory by a Christian military force since Muslim conquest in 711 A.D. Covadonga assured the survival of a Christian stronghold and today is regarded as the beginning of the Reconquista (recapture of Portugal & Spain). On 29 June 1236 A.D., after a siege of several months, Cordoba, Spain the capital of the Islam occupation of Spain was liberated by King Ferdinand III of Castile, Spain. Greece did not regain independence from the time of the fall of Constantinople in 1453 from the Muslim Empire until 1830. After World War II, in 1948 Israel became a nation again. The Muslim Empire made gains in 1947, Pakistan became an Islamic nation. And in the 1990's the Muslim Taliban took power in Afghanistan. In 2003 Saddam Hussein was ousted by Western forces and Iraq was liberated. The concerns of Islamic world ambition, Nuclear Iran, radical suicide bombers is a real concern to Western Civilization as evidenced by the following recent events:

- Plot to blow up passenger jets over the Atlantic Ocean by concealing liquid explosives in soft drink bottles was uncovered and prevented from taking place, Sep 7, 2009.

- Fort Hood, Army Base mass shooting, 12 killed, 31 wounded on November 5, 2009.

- Discover of the underwear bomber, Umar Farouk Abdulmutallab, with the explosive underwear worn on a Northwest airplane flight Dec 28, 2009.

- The New York police evacuated Times Square Saturday, after a crude car bomb of propane, gasoline and fireworks was discovered in a smoking Nissan Pathfinder in the heart of Times Square parked near Viacom headquarters, May 3, 2010.

In God we Trust all others pay Cash
– A Call to Action

We need to draw on creative ways to respond to the vanishing consumer worker model to avoid the collapse of western society, famine and suppression of the liberties of the survivors of western society by a take over of an oppressive government or foreign dictators. There can be an inspired solution. An inspired solution is the history of the United States. The United States is a unique experiment in the empowerment of the individual. Never before in the history of the world has the populace at large enjoyed the rights, liberties and opportunities as we now have and enjoy. These rights and privileges will be gone fast, as they are now rapidly evaporating with the elimination of the consumer worker model.

It is absolutely now the time to act before the opportunity to act is gone. In America our country was founded in freedom. Labor and serf labor have been eliminated. The consumer worker model replaced the oppressive models and obtained the prosperity shared by all. The next progression is the empowerment of the generation following the consumer workers. There are no jobs. Technology has overtaken the consumer worker model. Government cannot bring back jobs that been made obsolete by technology, through computers, robotics and artificial intelligence.

We can empower this generation by changing the economic system and not give all economic power to the government and the banks by simply developing and putting into practice the natural resource credit, which is an economic system that accounts for capital of private individuals while providing for ownership of the natural resources by the people. An accounting system that avoids the populace at large being the recipients of highly inflated worthless assets while the elitists are bailed out. Just as the early civilizations came into existence out of the fertilized fields from the overflowing of the Nile River so can western civilization progress from the consumer worker model to a technological society that would allow sharing the benefits of technology for all to self-fulfillment through academic and scientific achievement, through sports and through the development of the arts. It is a vast country with extensive natural resources and with the high technology in place today there is no reason for us to set back and watch it all evaporate when the answer can simply be found in economics.

Division of Labor or Class Warfare Theory & Key Words Definitions

Clearly individuals specializing in one task or another were able to improve, advance and produce higher quality and greater yield. The whole community benefited from the progress. A low cost source of food produced by a few became available to everyone in the community. Also a hierarchy developed. Decisions had to be made regarding ethics, principles and values, and also regarding planning, management and protection including the welfare of individuals. Three main divisions developed:

- Productive labor, working class/labor class —the human work necessary to produce goods and distribute them – Productive labor, may take the form of servitude, the worker is restrained and wholly dependent on his master for subsistence/shelter, a wage earner, paid money periodically for time worked, or an independent self-income producer tradesman/professional. The consumer worker falls under the wholly dependent wage earner. Primarily the consumer worker has been dependent on the mass employers for subsistence and shelter. Independents charge a fee based on their learned occupations, experience, standards of intellectual knowledge after education and training. Independents likely own the trade or professional implements. One of the aspects of labor is that the laborers do not own the factories or the land nor do they share in the profits.

- Warrior, members of the armed forces - The human work necessary to prepare for and to prevail in combat should the need arise. The conduct of military operations requires members of the armed forces to make extraordinary sacrifices, including the ultimate sacrifice, in order to provide for the common defense. Success in combat requires military units that are characterized by high morale, good order and discipline, and unit cohesion. Military life is fundamentally different from civilian life in that the extraordinary responsibilities of the armed forces, the unique conditions of military service, and that the military community, while subject to civilian control, exist as a specialized society; and the military society is characterized by its own laws, rules, customs, and traditions, including numerous restrictions on personal behavior, that would not be acceptable in civilian society. One of the aspects of being a member of the armed forces is that the members do not own the assets or the instrumentality of waging war, the weapons, hardware, or military facilities nor do the members share in the spoils of war.

- <u>Incoming/Outgoing Transitioning Individuals</u>. Two divisions of Transactional Individuals are individuals being displaced or displaced individuals or individual being integrated, integrated individuals a movement of individuals in or out of the society. Physically in the country but moving in/out or towards being an active member of the culture or loss of utility as a member, gain or loss of connection with the community, change of events, progress or recession leading to going out of usefulness, increase or loss of ability to provide/receive of gain or benefit. Independents likely own the trade or professional implements. One of the aspects of transitioning individuals is that these individuals can barely secure funds for their subsistence and shelter and clearly own no assets such as factories or land nor do they share in the profits.

- <u>Ruling Class - Government Policy-Makers</u> - Domestic and foreign policy makers, monetary policy makers and shapers of social legislation. The ruling class consists of Elitists, Business Tycoons & Banking Executives. One of the aspects of the ruling class is that the elitists, business tycoons & banking executives do own or direct the factories, the land, the natural resources, the money, share in and realize profits and direct the military in the common defense.

Key Words Definitions

- Banking Executives: The main purpose of high-ranking senior Banker Executives is to regulate the supply of money and credit to the economy. – Chairmen, Officers or owners of United States central bank and foreign central banks, and to a lesser degree domestic and foreign chartered banking institutions.

- Business Tycoons: Wealthy and powerful individuals in business, captains of industry, or wealthy merchants or industrialists.

- Class Warfare View: Those who control the capital, the capitalists in America versus the workers. Those who control the capital in America control and continue to enjoy ever increasing wealth. Capitalist continue to increase their wealth and influence through mercantilism. Politicized today, phony rhetoric to anger voters to vote for political character.

- Elitists: Upper class with social and economic power, high circles of power and influence. Characterized by far-reaching wealth or direct connection to such worldly possessions.

- Excise Tax: A tax on a specific good or service, regularly imposed on the quantity purchased rather than the value. Examples are gasoline taxes, cigarette taxes, and telecommunications taxes. Tax per gallon, tax per package, etc.

- Franchise: Authorization, a right or privilege granted to a person or group usually by the federal government. Example: motor vehicle assemblage franchise. Not just anyone can own a motor vehicle assemblage plant. The ownership of the franchise rights to manufacture automobiles is protected and concealed by the government. The government in the 1980's allowed foreign manufacturers to produce motor vehicles, Volkswagen and Toyota in the United States before issuing any more American owned franchises. The government in 2010 seized control and now operates two American vehicle assemblage plants, General Motors and Chrysler.

- Mercantilism: Roughly defined as the distribution of goods in order to realize a profit.

- Middle Class/Upper Class Jargon: Social stratification/Social classes theory taught in Sociology classes in the University, which gives everyone a false sense of elevation to the working class. Everyone considers himself or herself a member of the middle class. Politicians are always for benefits and tax cuts for the middle class, phony rhetoric to anger voters against the "upper class" to vote for political character.

- Natural Resource Credit: Amending the currency and monetary statutes to provide for credit on capital and wealth of private individuals in United States and for the American natural resources as credit to the American people individually, or as electricity at-large no charge, computing natural resource credits in the same way as an excise tax. Presently economic policy is one-sided producing inflation. Quantum Easing (QE), Digitizing Capital, and the velocity of money economic policies all boil down to one result: causing immediate inflation or deferred inflation, which is negative to the consumer worker. The natural resource credit offsets the value of the dollar against our natural recourses increasing the value of the American dollar, which increases the buying power of the consumer worker.

- Old Money: Families that have been wealthy for generations or members of such families, which is massive wealth obtained through exploitative industrialists and bankers, and, wealth protective income taxation to protect their old money from rival competition.

- Shareholders in America: As citizens we are all shareholders in America, as Thomas Jefferson described it "stake holders" because we all have a stake in America.

- Tariff Tax: A government tax on imports or exports.

- Quantitative easing (QE): A monetary policy to stimulate the economy. The money is "digitized" not printed. The central bank issues (creates) money, then electronically buys its own government bonds at a discount resulting in a yield (additional money) or electronically purchases other financial assets, in order to increase the money supply and the money reserves of the banking system, which also raises the value of the purchased financial assets.

- Quantum theory of money: Is to provide the quantity of money as needed in the American national economy. Money is a unit of measure and as more consumer workers labor earning money, depositing money, exchanging the money for consumables, as well as banks loaning money to consumer workers to finance purchases, so goes the velocity of money. The velocity of money (also known as the velocity of circulation) is the average frequency with which a unit of money is spent in a specific period of time. The quantum (quantity/ amount) theory (supply and demand) of money relates changes in price to changes in the quantity of money. Therefore the Federal Reserve Board theoretically controlling the printing of money controls inflation and deflation.

- Western Civilization: Western Civilization includes cultures, peoples, languages, and nations, whose economics stage is somewhere in the economic progression, family clans, city-states, feudal system, slave labor system, capital system, communism, industrial worker revolution, through today's consumer/worker model economics, which includes shared sacred knowledge, values and principles, passed on from the descendents of Noah, his three sons, Abraham, by and large the descendents of Abraham, including others as well who accepted the beliefs and values of the God of Abraham.

www.ingramcontent.com/pod-product-compliance
Lightning Source LLC
LaVergne TN
LVHW091200080426
835509LV00006B/758